MATTHEW MEAD'S
ULTIMATE
recycled
style
GUIDE

FOUNDER, CREATIVE DIRECTOR, EDITOR IN CHIEF Matthew Mead
MANAGING EDITOR Jennifer Mead
EXECUTIVE EDITOR Linda MacDonald
SENIOR EDITOR Sarah Egge
GRAPHIC DESIGNER Brian Michael Thomas/Our Hero Productions
STUDIO ASSISTANT/DESIGNER Lisa Bisson

With any craft project, check product labels to make sure that the materials you use are safe and nontoxic. The instructions in this book are intended to be followed with adult supervision.

NOTE: Neither the publisher nor the author is responsible for your specific health or allergy needs that may require medical supervision, or for any adverse reactions to the recipes contained in this book.

Matthew would like to thank everyone who contributed their time, talents, and/or invited us into their homes to help create this special volume, RECYCLED STYLE: Lisa Renauld, Mary and Gordon Welch, Marie and Everett Mead, Lee Repetto, Pat Turgeon, Donna Welch, The Lamp Shop, Tricia Foley, models Sophie MacDonald and Caroline Wills, Julie Merberg for her unyielding support, and the hard-working team at Time Home Entertainment, Inc.

PUBLISHER Jim Childs
VICE PRESIDENT, BUSINESS DEVELOPMENT & STRATEGY Steven Sandonato
EXECUTIVE DIRECTOR, MARKETING SERVICES Carol Pittard
EXECUTIVE DIRECTOR, RETAIL & SPECIAL SALES Tom Mifsud
EXECUTIVE PUBLISHING DIRECTOR Joy Butts
EDITORIAL DIRECTOR Stephen Koepp
EDITORIAL OPERATIONS DIRECTOR Michael Q. Bullerdick
DIRECTOR, BOOKAZINE DEVELOPMENT & MARKETING Laura Adam
FINANCE DIRECTOR Glenn Buonocore
ASSOCIATE PUBLISHING DIRECTOR Megan Pearlman
ASSISTANT GENERAL COUNSEL Helen Wan
ASSISTANT DIRECTOR, SPECIAL SALES Ilene Schreider
DESIGN & PREPRESS MANAGER Anne-Michelle Gallero
BRAND MANAGER, PRODUCT MARKETING Nina Fleishman
ASSOCIATE PREPRESS MANAGER Alex Voznesenskiy
ASSOCIATE PRODUCTION MANAGER Kimberly Marshall

SPECIAL THANKS Katherine Barnet, Jeremy Biloon, Susan Chodakiewicz, Rose Cirrincione, Lauren Hall Clark, Jacqueline Fitzgerald, Christine Font, Jenna Goldberg, Hillary Hirsch, Suzanne Janso, David Kahn, Mona Li, Amy Mangus, Robert Marasco, Amy Migliaccio, Nina Mistry, Dave Rozzelle, Ricardo Santiago, Adriana Tierno, Vanessa Wu

Published by Time Home Entertainment Inc.
135 West 50th Street • New York, NY 10020

ISBN 10: 0-8487-3444-0
ISBN 13: 978-0-8487-3444-2

We welcome your comments and suggestions about Time Home Entertainment Books. Please write to us at: Time Home Entertainment Books, Attention: Book Editors, P.O. Box 11016, Des Moines, IA 50336-1016

If you would like to order any of our hardcover Collector's Edition books, please call us at 1-800-327-6388, Monday through Friday, 7 a.m. to 8 p.m., or Saturday, 7 a.m. to 6 p.m., Central Time.

WE ALL HAVE A CONCEPT OF RECYCLING—whether it means hauling bottles to the curb at regular intervals or reusing plastic bags—but the term is truly a comprehensive one that goes well beyond daily chores. When my team and I were putting together this book over many months, we took the broad view of recycling, defined by Merriam-Webster as "to adapt to a new use." Transforming one thing into another, breathing new life into tired old wares became our mission. We shopped flea markets, thrift stores, garage sales, and even traded items with friends and neighbors to gather furnishings and accessories with potential beyond their current use. Along the way, we turned a garage into an entertaining space, rescued furniture that was headed to the dump, played with beautiful colors, threw a party, and turned up dozens of easy DIY projects. We proved that you can makeover an entire home, one room at a time, one lamp or stool at a time, with secondhand wares. And it doesn't have to look like a hodgepodge of stale styles. With paint or fabric embellishment, or just a thoughtful new use, old things can indeed be made fresh again—and modern and sophisticated and beautiful.

The process of recycling is a deeply personal one. What catches your eye is unique; how you choose to spiff it up and reuse it is a reflection of your tastes and talents. Let the inspiration, tips, techniques, and projects in **RECYCLED STYLE** help you express your individuality in your home. There's so much more to recycling than plastic bags. It offers a sure and inexpensive path to stylish living.

WHERE I SHOP FOR STYLE:

Goodwill Stores
Goodwill.org

Savers Thrift Stores
Savers.com

Salvation Army Thrift Stores
SalvationArmyUSA.org

Sage Farm Antiques, North Hampton, NH
SageFarmAntiques.com

Todd Farm Flea Market, Rowley, MA
ToddFarm.com

From Out of the Woods Antiques, Goffstown, NH
FromOutOfTheWoodsAntiques.com

Milford Antique Show, Milford, NH
MilfordAntiquesShow.com

SoWa Vintage Market, Boston, MA
SoWaVintageMarket.com

MATTHEW MEAD'S
ULTIMATE
recycled style
GUIDE

110

142

194

SETTING UP SHOP

Use repurposed items to create a work space where you can fix, clean, and make items using all of your "recycled" finds. Read on as Matthew shares his tips, tricks, and favorite products for transforming almost anything into a useful treasure.

re-imagine

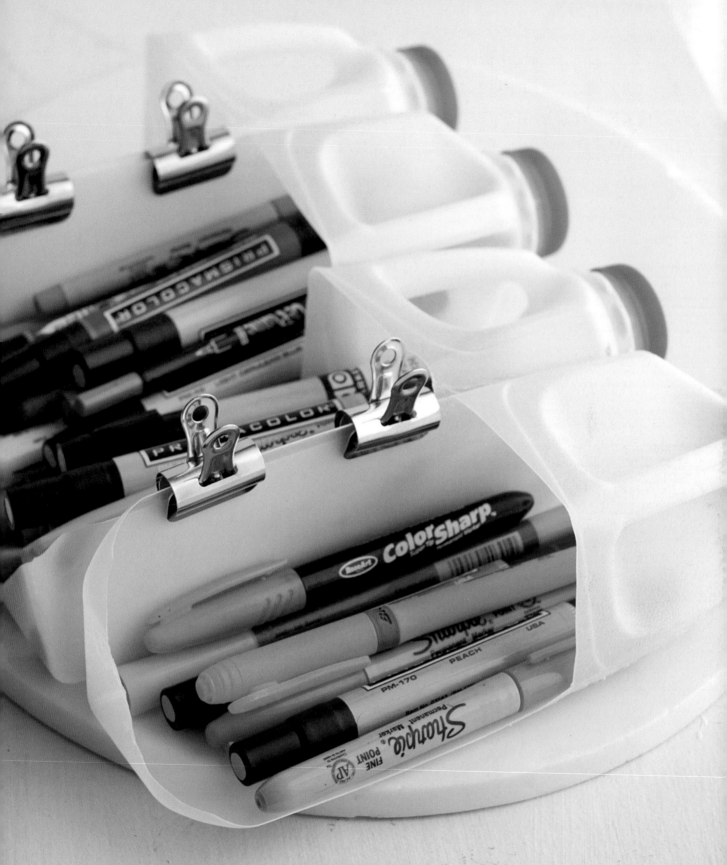

ORDERLY FASHION

Matthew re-glued and painted an old expandable kitchen table (OPPOSITE) and added wheels to it to create a rolling island that is perfect for working on a variety of projects, both large and small. "I discovered some automotive cabinetry on Craig's List for a song," explains Matthew, "and I use it to store all of my tools for crafting and repairing, as well as some vintage supplies that I will repurpose as cards, gift tags, and even art." Recycled milk cartons (ABOVE) are cut out to corral and organize markers by color.

IF TAKING OVER YOUR DINING ROOM TABLE as a creative work space (only to have to clear it all off again come dinner time!) just isn't cutting it any longer, consider creating a stand-alone space where you can re-use, re-purpose and re-imagine your favorite finds. Carving out just such a spot—whether it be in an alcove, a basement, or tucked away in a sunny corner of your porch—will not only bring order to your efforts, but also make the creative process more fun. And with years of experience in churning out projects worthy of publication, it is a tried and true tip that Matthew swears by: "Devoting a space to use solely for creative endeavors is not only fun but necessary to prevent the negative effect that disorder can have on the creative process. I simply work better in an organized environment, one where my tools and supplies are within reach—allowing me to easily complete the projects I dream up. And keeping the things I need nearby allows me to engage any transformation at a moment's notice." When creating your own studio, craft station, or work table, gather up vintage or empty containers to hold paint brushes, tape, and twine. Create different stations and use everyday objects to organize and display materials and supplies by color and function. "I think of the process of 'setting up shop' as the ultimate exercise in re-purposing everything," confides Matthew.

LIKE WITH LIKE

Group similar items together for easy access: **1.** Fill drawers with task-related supplies like miniature paint brushes, colored pencils, and scissors. **2.** Rinse out and fill used mustard, jam, and baby food jars with your favorite paint colors for eye-catching style. **3.** Store rolls of gift wrap in a screened galvanized basket. **4.** Why shouldn't organization be beautiful? Seaside finds hold court in a charming array of vintage plant pots to create an inspiring tableau.

1

2

3

STORAGE ISSUES

Handy storage is where it's at and cupboards—either wooden or metal—can be a wonderful way to keep everything handy and organized (OPPOSITE). "I like that there is a place for everything and everything is in its own place," says Matthew. "It means I can always find what I need at a glance, freeing up my time so that I can create new things or head out on a hunt for treasures."

THIS PAGE: **1.** A folding cutting-mat can be stored easily or placed out on a table top and covered with glass for an exacting cutting surface. **2.** Old berry boxes, in quart and pint sizes, hold ribbons of varying colors and lengths. **3.** Vintage pottery and old baskets become pretty containers to store scissors, seam binding, and threads of all kinds.

"Twenty years as a thrifty collector and recycler has provided me with an abundance of tips and tricks for creating marvellous projects using mundane objects."
— Matthew

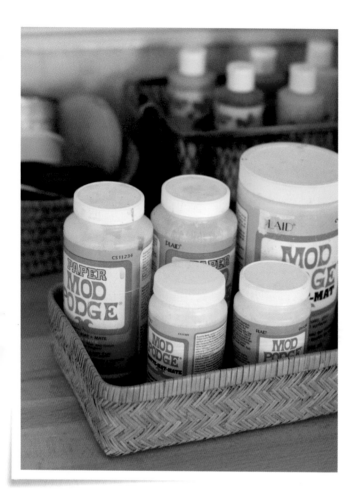

Matthew's go-to products for:

CRAFTS

"I am mad about ribbon, acrylic paint, and Mod Podge®, which comes in multiple finishes, cleans up with water, and is a dream for any découpage project—from papering a room divider in ephemera to creating a memory plate that can be hung on a wall. I keep multiple glues and adhesives together in one basket, but my Mod Podge® gets a wicker tray all of its own," says Matthew.

COLLECTIBLES

A thorough cleaning is a must for any item that you plan to repurpose. "I have assembled a 'war chest' when it comes to reclaiming the original, natural beauty of an item," admits Matthew. He stocks this chest with cotton swabs, which are great for cleaning cracks and creases in furniture, on glass, or porcelain. Old toothbrushes are the best way to scrub off dirt and grime from old bottles or clay items that have been outside. A bleach pen is great for removing stains on contemporary fabrics that you might find at thrift stores and yard sales. Goo Gone® and Goof Off® can be used to remove sticky label residue, dried paint, scuff marks, and oil stains. Matthew uses furniture polish to lightly revive and brighten items that need a visual boost, but not actual refinishing. Finally, a good scouring powder will whiten and brighten items made of porcelain and ironstone.

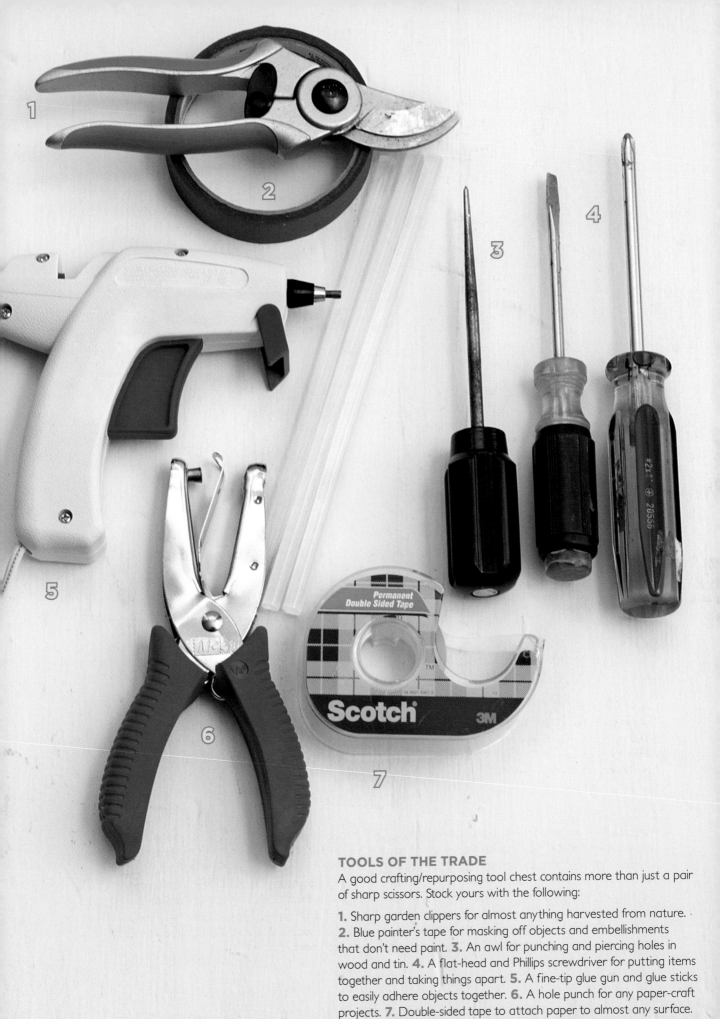

TOOLS OF THE TRADE

A good crafting/repurposing tool chest contains more than just a pair of sharp scissors. Stock yours with the following:

1. Sharp garden clippers for almost anything harvested from nature.
2. Blue painter's tape for masking off objects and embellishments that don't need paint. **3.** An awl for punching and piercing holes in wood and tin. **4.** A flat-head and Phillips screwdriver for putting items together and taking things apart. **5.** A fine-tip glue gun and glue sticks to easily adhere objects together. **6.** A hole punch for any paper-craft projects. **7.** Double-sided tape to attach paper to almost any surface.

UPCYCLE STYLE

All it takes to transform secondhand and thrifted items into a cohesive look is close-at-hand tools and tips from an expert. Enter Matthew. He'll show you how he put together this romantic cottage look for bottom dollar.

BLUSH OF COLOR

To turn a $5 tray into a fetching memory board (OPPOSITE), Matthew sprayed it white, then hand-painted a border using pink acrylic paint. A platter hanger attaches it to the wall. This sunroom (THIS PAGE) has new verve thanks to a bright 1930's pantry cabinet—$35—that Matthew painted and papered in trendy cerise pink.

"STYLE IS ALL ABOUT turning everyday items into something pretty," Matthew says. "We used to call it 'making-do,' but upcycling has a much better ring to it!" When you can "make-do" on the cheap with furnishings that are easy to find—it's perfect bliss, he says. At the flea markets and secondhand and thrift stores Matthew routinely scours, there is an endless supply of home décor that is rarely ready for a magazine photo shoot. That's when his skills at upcycling come in handy. His favorite tool is a paintbrush, because he says he can transform just about anything with a new coat of paint. He also keeps a stash of pretty papers, from leftover wallpaper bits to holiday cards to packages of crafts-store scrapbook paper. Various adhesives, including wood glue and hot glue (and his current favorite: glue dots) are necessary materials. The rest is determined by what he sees in the piece he picks up. "There's never a plan for what I buy or how—exactly—I'll use it," he says. "I just pick something, picture the possibilities in my mind, and then play around until it all works out."

ON EXHIBIT
One of Matthew's favorite finds at a garage sale or flea market is a plain wood box (OPPOSITE). Here, he dressed up three $10-$20 boxes with new paint and glued-on molding details, and then stacked them for handy storage. An $8 jar is never just a jar: It can be a vase, a jug for lemonade, a light fixture, and a displayer of interesting bits and baubles. These balls of twine (ABOVE, LEFT), for example, take on an artistic presence. The $2 hanging basket (ABOVE, RIGHT) returns to decorative status with a wash of color and new function as a wall vase. "Simple baskets in any shape and form are great finds and often cost less than $5 apiece," Matthew says.

HOW TO GET THE LOOK

To turn your finds into fabulous treasures, try these ideas: **1.** Double-stick tape secures a piece of giftwrap to the cupboard door. **2.** Glue magnets to small dishes using Liquid Nails®, then affix number decals. **3.** A wash of color (1 part paint to 2 parts water) gently updates pieces while keeping some patina. **4.** A color wash also adds age to new trims.

OPPOSITE: No wiring! Stick a halogen puck light to a lampshade using heavy-duty carpet tape, then suspend from twine. See how it adds flair outdoors in Camping Chic, page 220.

SOMETHING OLD
WEDDING PRESENTS

If gifting from an impersonal registry gives you cold feet, try thrifting instead. Vintage items are valuable and meaningful, and they may inspire a lifelong collection for the couple.

COLORED GLASSWARE is easy to find at garage sales and antique stores. Pick a shade, such as the bride's wedding hue, and amass a variety (ABOVE) that can be used as vases or as a centerpiece arrangement. Sterling silver has long been an elegant, tasteful wedding gift. It is, however, a bit hard on the wallet to buy new pieces. By purchasing items such as this candy bowl (OPPOSITE) secondhand from a rummage sale, you save the cost and gain patina.

HEARTFELT MEMENTOES

With recycled items, it's easy to picture a new bride generations ago unfurling the embroidered tablecloth over her table, or polishing the same silver candlestick. These presents are sentimental links to joyful moments that have come before. **1.** A gift that suggests closeness, these ivory spoons are playful and hardworking at the same time. The couple can use them when entertaining or just as part of their morning coffee routine. **2.** Decorative small vases are handy gifts. This Bristol glass vase features delicate hand painting and wears a few marks of time. Pen a gift card that wishes the couple the same longevity together. **3.** Hand-stitched linens are a meaningful present. Each one displays the love of its creator. The linens speak of special occasions, such as hosting the new in-laws or celebrating an anniversary, but they're hardy enough for everyday use as well.

OPPOSITE: Mismatched candlesticks are easier to find—and more charmingly unique—than a matched set.

TIP: To distinguish silver pieces from silver-plate (a thin veneer of silver over a lesser metal), look for a "sterling" stamp somewhere on the piece.

"Jenny and I treasure the wedding gifts
we received almost 20 years ago. Each
one recalls a memory or feeling of
contentment. These gifts will, too."
— Matthew

RAISE A GLASS
Celery glasses (THIS PAGE), which are elongated goblets for serving crudité, are fun, versatile gifts. They can hold tea lights, stock silverware at a party, or serve as the couple's toasting glasses. The compote (OPPOSITE) has a celebratory quality, like putting something on a pedestal. The bride can fill it with her bouquet flowers or mementoes from the couple's honeymoon.

SHINE ON

Trade in your crusty, smelly bottle of silver polish for a bit of baking powder. All you need is elbow grease to make the finish sparkle like new.

WHAT YOU'LL NEED:

O Tarnished silver or silver-plate items

O Cool water

O Baking Powder

O Sponge

O Soft, clean cotton cloth

STEP ONE Old pieces of sterling silver and silver-plate look terrible when they're tarnished and dingy. As a result, they can often be steals at thrift stores and garage sales. But under that grime is genuine value, if you're willing to scrub for it.

STEP TWO Fill a basin with cool tap water and soak the piece of silver or silver-plate. (If the piece is large, work in portions and wet as you go.) Pull the dripping piece out, sprinkle on a thick dusting of baking powder, and use a damp sponge to work the powder into a paste that covers the metal.

STEP THREE Let the piece dry with the baking powder set on its surface, which takes about 20 minutes. Run the piece under water to remove the dried powder, then buff gently with a soft cloth to restore shine (OPPOSITE).

DISHING IT UP

Easy to find and also a bargain, plates and dishes make wonderful decorative accessories for a variety of home décor projects. And the best part? You can pick a color palette and collect endless shapes, styles, and sizes—and revel in how these unique pieces come together so beautifully.

PLATE GALLERY
Take your plates out of the kitchen: You can create a striking wall arrangement by varying the shapes and sizes of the plates but sticking to the same color palette. Lay the plates out on the floor, and find a pleasing overall pattern before hanging them on the wall.

YOU CAN'T GET MUCH MORE OF A BARGAIN at a flea market or thrift shop than dishes, and no one knows that better than Matthew. Whether used simply to set a pretty table or for use in creative repurposing projects, their affordable price makes them an irresistible purchase just about everywhere he goes. And they don't have to be perfect to catch his eye. "Even discount stores and manufacturer's seconds work well as decorative shelf pieces, " he advises. "Small cracks, chips, and minor damage are typically benign in nature when you are planning to use the pieces for display." Collecting such dishes can also become a happy scavenger hunt as you rummage through church fairs, tag sales, and thrift shops to find additional pieces to a pattern or various sizes that can be combined to form a graduated set. Matthew likes transferware in a myriad of styles and colors and they are his go-to collection for both decorating and entertaining purposes. "Table-top pieces in intricate patterns and designs hold such allure for me," says Matthew. "I like having a diverse mix of serving pieces, but I also enjoy using plates and platters to corral clutter like our keys and mail or for use as a base for pillar-candle groupings." Affordable and diverse, decorating with dishes is truly a beautiful union of form and function.

STAND AND DELIVER

Graduated platters or plates make great serving stands. To make one easily, use wine or cordial glasses to create the central stand and attach to the underside of the plate using tacky wax (you can find this sticky wax at hardware stores or the display-booth supply area of your favorite antiques shop). Assemble and use to display cookies, candy, or even table favors at a shower or wedding.

AT YOUR SERVICE

If you have a china cupboard or butler's pantry filled with unused pieces, bring them out and put them to work: **1.** A bowl and oversized mug work together to dish out botanical bath salts in the bathroom. **2.** Compotes, tureens, pedestal dishes, and saucers can bring organization to a desk or entry way. Use them to hold mail, photos, or to keep a stack of appointment reminders and post cards within easy reach. **3.** Layer a large plate or platter with old finger bowls or sauce vessels and fill each with water and single blooms for a fool-proof dining or coffee-table arrangement. For more prominent centerpieces, fill larger bowls with fresh white roses, trumping the need for the more expected vase.

> " I am drawn to blue and white transferware dishes, but other classic color combinations are also in demand. "
> — Matthew

BOWLED OVER

Often, when patterned sets become separated, they sell for very little money. Find these pieces at yard sales and thrift stores for mere pennies on the dollar and use them as part of a mismatched set or for repurposing projects. Get to know when half-price days at your local thrift shop are held and mark your calendar for deep discounts on amazing pieces.

OVER EASY

If it can hold water, then it can readily become a charming vase, no matter its shape or size. This diminutive egg cup is perfect for a cluster of hydrangea blossoms. Use alone to dress up a dinner tray, the side of a bathroom sink, or amass a collection of egg cups and dot the top of your table with both flowers and tea lights.

SHELF HELP
Plates can be used as pretty wall accessories in many ways. Use a turkey platter as a bedside table with the help of sturdy, decorative wall brackets. To make, simply paint utility brackets to match your wall color and affix to the wall using screws and anchors. Top with the platter, which can be held in place using large pieces of tacky wax or Fun-Tak mounting putty. Arrange with books, flowers, or light-weight technology.

MIXING BOWLS

Once you begin a collection (OPPOSITE), it is fun to see how different pattern motifs and hues can work together. A set of graduated bowls can come together to make a beautiful floral cachepot. Make your own using porcelain egg cups or glass votive holders as risers (ABOVE). Hold the pedestals in place with tacky wax and then fill each level with water decanted from a pitcher. Tuck in your favorite fresh flowers (RIGHT) for a unique centerpiece, or as a way to dress up a sideboard.

step-by-step
bright idea

Follow these step-by-step instructions to create your own one-of-a-kind custom lamp using recycled finds, graphic wallpaper or gift wrap, and a simple lamp kit.

> "Lamps are special to me and I love to create unique ones using found objects that catch my eye and then top them off with a striking shade."
> — Matthew

WHAT YOU'LL NEED:

- ○ A lamp or vase and lamp-kit
- ○ A strong adhesive such as Liquid Nails®
- ○ 3 square-feet of patterned paper
- ○ Scissors and pencil
- ○ 15-20 binder clips
- ○ Lamp arc and rings

STEP ONE For the lamp base, use a recycled lamp or install lamp hardware into a vase or bottle using a lamp kit from LampShop.com. Matthew found this mercury glass bottle at a flea market, where he also picked up the wooden platform base that he painted black.

STEP TWO When using a vase for your lamp, follow the lamp kit manufacturer's directions to assemble the electrical components. Once together as a unit, the rubber-stopper socket set fits snugly into the vase or bottle opening and the vase cap will hide the unattractive stopper.

STEP THREE Use Liquid Nails® (or epoxy glue) to attach the wooden base to the bottom of the lamp or vase. Let dry according to the manufacturer's directions.

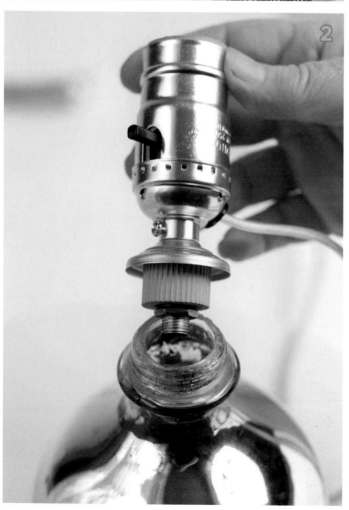

STEP FOUR When using a lamp kit, choose one with a cord that leads off the socket itself, eliminating the need to drill a hole in the lamp base. LampShop.com is an excellent source for all of the components you will need to repurpose or create a show-stopping lamp.

STEP FIVE To create the lampshade, measure the height of the lamp base (and its harp, if it has one) to help you choose the desired style and size of shade. Using the height and circumference measurements of the shade frame, draw an arc onto craft paper to create the lampshade template.

STEP SIX Trace the template onto the patterned wallpaper or gift wrap of your choice and cut out the shade using scissors. Next, use a product called pressure-sensitive adhesive styrene (which is a vellum-like material with a sticky surface on one side). Peel the paper backing from the styrene, lay the gift wrap or wallpaper arc on it, and then cut out the arc once again. The styrene provides stiffness to the gift wrap, creating a more sturdy and durable lampshade.

STEP SEVEN To create the finished shade, simply attach the arc to the lamp shade rings (which are provided with most arc and shade kits). Clip the arc to the rings using binder clips.

STEP EIGHT Attach binder clips just along the edges of both the top and bottom rings so that you have a fully-formed shade. Using a pencil, lightly mark the seam of the shade along the vertical line where the paper ends meet.

STEP NINE Remove the binder clips and place glue along the underside of the pencil mark as you prepare to secure the ends together.

TIP: When purchasing or assembling a lamp kit for this project, be sure it includes a socket, cord set, rubber stopper, washers, and vase cap.

STEP TEN Place the seam end of the paper just at the pencil line, and then smooth to secure the seam. Let dry 10 minutes.

STEP ELEVEN Glue in the top and bottom rings. Place glue on each ring and place just inside of the shade. Wipe away excess glue and hold rings in place with several binder clips. Let dry for 30 minutes or more.

STEP TWELVE To trim the shade, you may use paper tape, ribbon, seam binding, or vintage trim. Matthew trimmed his shade using the same gift wrap used for the shade. Using the shade circumference as a guide, cut long strips of paper about 2 ¾ inches wide to make a paper tape. Use glue to adhere the tape to the top and bottom of the shade. Place paper tape on the edge of the shade so that half the tape will horizontally trim the shade and the other portion with be glued and folded over just beneath the edges of the shade.

STEP THIRTEEN Let dry thoroughly and attach the shade to the light bulb using a bulb adapter. The finished lamp is a crisp and updated light fixture that will brighten any room with style – day or night.

MINIATURE GARDENS

Like tiny new blooms that peek forth from the snow, container gardens are popping up everywhere. Search the flea market for unique containers and add in some early-bird plants for instant spring color.

NOTHING ANNOUNCES THE ARRIVAL OF SPRING more than the appearance of spring favorites like daffodils, hyacinths, tulips, and pansies. And timed perfectly with that is the return of outdoor flea markets, tag sales, and the popular thirty (plus)-mile yard sales. While scanning the tables at these sales, glance down at the ground for unique containers and pots that are hard at work holding other items, and look at old objects in new ways to determine if they can serve as alternative vessels that can be used inside or out. Glass jars can become instant terrariums, deep galvanized metal trays and sap buckets (ABOVE) can hold an abundance of plants, and weathered pots offer rustic balance to the colorful new blooms of your favorite spring flowers.

PURPLE PERSUASION

Terrariums can be closed or open (uncovered) like this one planted in a tall glass jar (OPPOSITE) found at a tag sale. Just be sure to pair plants with similar watering needs and add a layer of drainage material before adding enough soil to cover the roots. A mixture of grape hyacinths, violas, and pansies shares space with a lettuce plant that can be trimmed back to avoid overcrowding. Ensure the soil remains just slightly moist—never bone dry—and place in an area that provides natural, indirect sunlight.

Pink and yellow primrose plants, kalanchoe, gold-tip spiked moss, and mini daffodils bring color to a grouping of old pots, platters, and urns collected over time for just a few dollars each.

IN LIVING COLOR

A weathered pot (ABOVE) is softened by a generous planting of pansies, scabiosa (in back), and arabis. The cool monochromatic palette complements the aged patina of the old vessel. OPPOSITE: Find old sap cans for a song at flea markets and yard sales. Drill holes in the bottom for drainage and revive them with a wash of latex paint in a cheerful hue. Line the can with 1-2 inches of pea gravel, and then fill them with potting soil and a bouquet of vibrant spring blooms.

Go for a full-on monochromatic palette by matching the flower color to that of the container.

FLOWER BASKET
Fill an old basket with a bevy of blooms like this assortment of miniature daffodils, phlox, pansies, and ivy. To prevent soil run-off and allow for adequate drainage, line the basket with sphagnum moss or a polyethylene liner (with drainage holes poked in it) before planting.

GARDEN VARIETY

Look for curious objects to use as vessels for container plants, like this old farm sieve (ABOVE). Filled with miniature daffodils, hydrangea, and primrose plants, it is a perfect home with built-in drainage holes (drill extra holes in the bottom of the container if needed).

CONTAINER GARDEN

Choosing container plants goes beyond your personal preference: For optimal compatibility, take note of each plant's light needs, color, foliage, and its maximum growth.

WHAT YOU'LL NEED:

- ○ A variety of early-season flowering plants (see pages 50–51 for the plant varieties used here)

- ○ Shallow galvanized metal container

- ○ Small stones for drainage

- ○ Indoor potting soil

- ○ Medium-sized polished stones to cover soil

STEP ONE Cover the bottom of a 6-8 inch-high galvanized metal or glass container with a generous drainage layer of pea gravel or packaged pea stones from a florist or craft store.

STEP TWO Fill with a layer of indoor potting soil. Make small wells in the soil for each plant. Temporarily arrange each plant until you achieve a pleasing overall shape. For best results, situate tall plants, like the miniature daffodils, in the center of the container. Separate flowers that are the same color, and mix in plants with different foliage texture.

STEP THREE Begin placing the plants in the container, first removing their original pots, and add enough soil to cover all roots. Fill in empty spots with smaller plants. For a tried-and-true formula, combine trailing, upright, and filler plants in every container garden.

STEP FOUR Finish with a top layer of medium-sized stones for a more polished effect and a natural "mulch." Water thoroughly according to the plants' needs.

COOKING UP STYLE

Serve up fresh style with a mini kitchen-makeover that calls for a sprinkling of flea market finds, a dash of color, and an ounce of ingenuity. By mixing tasteful design and function, you'll uncover the recipe for reinvention.

HIT REFRESH
Revitalize your kitchen with an infusion of color and repurposed finds. Here, old country work tables serve as prep stations and an island; pull up vintage industrial stools to sit on. For unique art, spell out culinary words using stickers on old platters.

SMART SALVAGE
This former laboratory sink (BELOW) can be used for washing dishes or arranging flowers and tending plants. It's salvaged finds like this—and the old metal brackets that hold a cast-off piece of marble—that make a kitchen makeover affordable and unique.

DUAL PURPOSE

Elevate everyday items with flair: **1.** Arrange colorful cleaning supplies on a stand for easy access. **2.** Place a variety of scouring pads in a compote lined with pea stones. **3.** Tote napkins to the table in a glass compote. **4.** Fill a cake stand with oils and spices.

ON DISPLAY

1. Search flea markets for damaged tables with marble tops to repurpose as elegant cutting boards or serving platters. **2.** A vintage laundry basket on wheels can be used to corral fruits or vegetables. Top it with a wooden lid from an old crock. **3.** A wire baker's basket is an easy way to store and transport commonly used kitchen items, like these yellow-ware bowls and wooden cutting boards. **4.** Stack everyday dishware and serving pieces on cake stands to free up counter space.

Vintage bowls inspire the color redo of an old wood shelf that sits bottoms-up on the counter. To get the look, mix up chalk paint: 1 part plaster of Paris to 2 parts paint. Then thin with water as desired.

OPEN STORAGE

To create a kitchen with elements that can be changed up easily, choose utilitarian pieces that reflect your decorative style. Display often-used items on open shelving and hooks—like these vintage copper pots (ABOVE) that can be found readily at estate sales, thrift shops, and flea markets. Store necessities that aren't attractive, like paper towels and trash bags, in covered baskets or hampers (see page 60), crock pots, or tucked away in drawers.

ON THE MOVE

Fill an old metal mop bucket with a bevy of apricot roses and hydrangea blooms. Alternatively, line the bucket with a florist's container and fill with ice for a portable beverage vessel. Wheel it from room to room or place atop the kitchen island for impact.

step-by-step
art revival

Embrace the past and present by making copies of old family artwork using your camera, a color printer, and some heavy-weight paper. Finish it off with a dusting of colorful glitter.

WHAT YOU'LL NEED:

- ○ A painting or print
- ○ Camera paper
- ○ Double-sided matte brochure paper
- ○ Artistic pastel chalks
- ○ Make-up applicator
- ○ Various colors of fine glitter
- ○ Mod Podge® or white glue
- ○ Small paintbrush

"With today's technology, it is possible to make copies of treasured family paintings so that each relative can share in a special heirloom."
— Matthew

STEP ONE Photograph and print the artwork onto a sheet of 8.5 × 11-inch double-sided matte brochure paper. Assemble pastel chalks in a variety of shades to use for highlighting and enhancing the colors of the print.

STEP TWO Vintage pieces often fade from years of exposure to light, and a scan or photograph may appear even less clear. Apply the pastel chalk colors with a make-up applicator to restore some vibrancy to the image.

STEP THREE Prepare a glitter station: glitter will highlight the details of the artwork while adding dimension and sparkle. Assemble a selection of colored glitter, Mod Podge®, and a small liner paintbrush on a tray or cookie sheet.

STEP FOUR Use the small paintbrush to outline and highlight the painting with Mod Podge® (or glue).

STEP FIVE Apply the glitter. Here, we placed glue along the dark edges of the flowers and leaves and then lightly sprinkled the glue with glitter.

STEP SIX Turn the paper on its edge and tap it onto the tray to remove the excess glitter.

STEP SEVEN Clean off the tray when changing glitter colors. Repeat steps five and six when applying glitter to each different detail you choose to embellish. Let dry overnight, then dust excess glitter from the finished piece using a clean paintbrush.

SHARED SENTIMENT For special occasions, use your printer to make miniature prints that can be used as stylish gift tags for pretty packages. Family members, in particular, will love this tiny nod to the past.

PRIVATE PARKING

Looking for a little extra lounging or entertaining space?
Head to the garage. With salvaged materials, refurbished
furnishings, and some elbow grease, you can create an
al fresco living space as charming as this one that's just
steps from Matthew and Jenny's back door.

JUST LIKE HOME
To accomplish a convincing makeover, erase
all thoughts of the space as a garage. Think
of it instead as a soon-to-be great room.
Then give the windows, walls, and floor the
same decorative attention as you would any
other room in your home.

MATTHEW AND JENNY ADORE the cozy confines of their early-1900s bungalow where they raised their children and have lived for 12 years. But like all mid-size homes, it isn't blessed with bonus spaces—the kind of living and lounging rooms that let them enjoy time together reading or updating Pinterest boards, or where they can spread out big projects or have cocktails with friends. So, last summer, they embarked on a redo in the garage to gain a three-season living room. They moved the cars to the driveway, relocated stored items to a backyard shed, and gave the space a good scrubbing. First they refreshed the dingy surfaces with paint. The wood walls were primed with a stain-blocking oil-based primer, then sprayed with a crisp white latex paint, which brightens the space. The concrete base of the walls and the floor were coated in water-base paints that are formulated for concrete and garage floors. The charcoal gray hue on the floor conceals any previous stains. A carpenter built a long shelf between two windows, and he erected the screened wall that keeps the space comfortably bug-free. For that, Matthew and Jenny provided a hodgepodge of items they'd been gathering at flea markets, including a screen door. Finally, the fun part: They furnished the space with furniture bought as seconds and from local thrift stores. By keeping the palette strictly white, gray, and black (inspired by Matthew's framed photos) they could spiff up wood pieces with paint as needed. A few interesting accessories and collections flesh out the space and make it feel like a seamless—and welcoming—extension of their home.

PHOTO FINISH
Matthew printed some favorite images from his photography work and placed them in crafts-store black frames (ABOVE, LEFT). Placed atop a luggage stand, a galvanized tray becomes a handy bar (ABOVE, RIGHT). A large gray area rug defines the seating group.

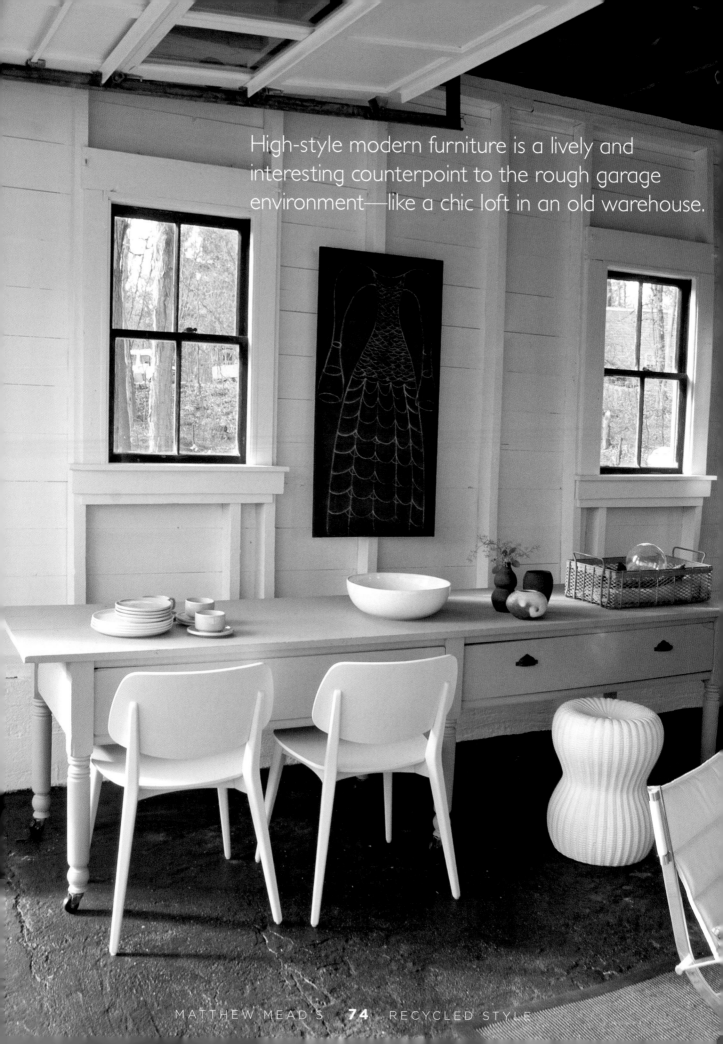

High-style modern furniture is a lively and interesting counterpoint to the rough garage environment—like a chic loft in an old warehouse.

MODERN MELD

Mid-century bentwood chairs pull up to a long farmhouse table (OPPOSITE), which can be a desk, crafting surface, or dining table. Everything in the garage came from different flea markets, seconds stores, and thrift shops, but the pieces work harmoniously thanks to the restricted color palette.. Black garden ornaments pop against the white walls (ABOVE).

1 2

3

STYLE NOTES

You can stop at just paint and furniture in a bonus room, but it's the additional layer of meaningful items that make it a true living space. **1.** A rectangular accent pillow softens the curve of this sophisticated chair. **2.** Large floor pillows are handy cushions or extra seating for a crowd. To make each one, Jenny cut two 20 x 20-inch squares of felt (which won't fray). Using her sewing machine, she sewed straight stitches with colorful embroidery floss as a border on one. Then she sewed the two pieces together around the perimeter, leaving an opening for stuffing. Once filled, she hand-sewed the opening closed. **3.** Browsing books are always handy. This stool was a discount-store find.

TIP: For art-on-the-cheap, snap a photo of a simple subject, such as your pet's face, your baby's feet, or a sunflower. Enlarge and print it at a copy store, and hang it using an inexpensive poster frame from the crafts store.

CROWD PLEASERS

Larger than any room in their house, the garage offers Matthew and Jenny a place to entertain a crowd comfortably. In addition to the obvious chairs and sofa, they snuck in extra seating spots with a stool, floor pillows, and the coffee table, which is actually a bench.

EXTRA FUNCTION
With such a large space, Matthew was able to divide it into zones: one for seating and another as a small workspace. This desk and chair take advantage of the natural light of one of the garage's windows. The ladder that used to access storage above the rafters is now a decorative element.

SCREEN WALL

Flying, biting insects make living outdoors in the summer a challenge in most neighborhoods. That makes a screen wall a good choice for a garage transformation. To keep the pests out, and you and your guests comfortable within, read on:

WHAT YOU'LL NEED:

- ○ Salvaged building materials, such as doors and brackets
- ○ Lumber
- ○ Fabric screen
- ○ Wire mesh
- ○ White paint
- ○ Concrete fasteners
- ○ Wood shelf brackets from the home center
- ○ Wood corbels from the home center

STEP ONE For the door everyone uses to come and go, Matthew and Jenny found a flea-market screen door with style cues that place it in the Victorian era. It needed a little TLC to be hardy enough for today's use. A sturdy wood finial replaces the handle. And thin screen fabric is reinforced with heavy-duty metal mesh.

STEP TWO To mimic the curvy vintage brackets on the vintage screen door, Matthew and Jenny chose simpler new versions from the home center. These pine brackets define the upper sections of the screen wall. More substantial pine corbels are used in the lower sections. Both styles cost less than $10 apiece.

STEP THREE The new framework for the screen wall was built within and attached to the existing framing for the garage door opening.

STEP FOUR When the garage door is retracted, it disappears from view. When it is lowered, it doesn't interfere with the screen wall.

STEP FIVE To attach the screen wall framing to the driveway, metal L-brackets were secured with galvanized flat-head concrete screws, which won't rust when exposed to the elements.

A screen wall with divided panels looks attractive—especially with wood brackets defining the corners of each section—but it also secures the flimsy screen fabric better. The wood supports offer more places to anchor the screening, so it won't sag over time.

DESK SET

All you need is a free corner in any room to create an oasis of a workspace. Watery colors and verdant elements of the natural world combine to quench your creative thirsts.

WATER WORKS

Pick a theme, then carry it through. **1.** Tokens of the ocean appear in a shell and tramp-art pedestal. **2.** Showcase blooms in sea-hue bottles—both vintage and new. **3.** Boost the palette with thrift-store vessels. **4.** An easy-care terrarium adds perpetual freshness.

CUT 'N' PASTE

Personalize a plain Jane photo frame with this simple découpage technique. Cut pieces of patterned scrapbook paper to adhere around the edge of the frame with clear-drying glue.

WHAT YOU'LL NEED:

- ○ Old picture frame
- ○ Scrapbook paper
- ○ Scissors or an Xacto® knife
- ○ ModPodge® découpage medium
- ○ 1-inch foam brush
- ○ Ruler or straightedge

STEP ONE Matthew repurposed a photo frame with a wide, flat surface so he could show off the patterned scrapbook paper. First, he measured the dimensions of the surface of the frame, as well as the inner edges and outer edges, and transferred them to the scrapbook paper to cut 12 separate strips.

STEP TWO With the strips cut, he brushed a thin layer of découpage medium on one part of the frame at a time. Then he applied the paper to the clear-drying glue, smoothing it with his fingers. He repeated the process with all parts until the frame was covered. Finally, he brushed a coat of découpage medium over the entire paper-covered frame as a sealant, and let it dry.

TIP: Popular since the Victorian era, découpage is a crafting technique anyone can master. To make this photo-frame project kid-friendly, let little hands tear the paper into scraps then glue the pieces on randomly like a collage.

MEADOW MERRIMENT

Eager to surprise a dear friend with a birthday celebration, Matthew and Jenny set the scene in a tucked away, sunlit corner of a grassy meadow. Colorfully painted flea-market furniture, cheery fabric remnants, and sweet treats combine to create a charming al fresco party.

BLOOMING SWEET
Nearby poppies inspired these pretty cupcakes. Iced in the same citrusy hues found on the rustic wooden table and benches—and topped with fondant poppy blooms—they make a sweet offering when presented on vintage porcelain plates.

FOTO MAT

Create your own photo booth by gathering fun theatrical props for your guests to dress up in and have their photograph taken. Matthew put out vintage top hats, canes, a colorful parasol as well as lampshades and photo bubbles for guests to create long lasting take home mementos of the party.

An old country table, revived with a wash of orange paint, moves from truck to meadow where it holds an open-air buffet of cookies and field strawberries.

PUNCH OF COLOR

An old glass rose bowl from the thrift shop is repurposed as a
perfect punch bowl and filled with a refreshing blend of orange juice,
pineapple nectar, lemon seltzer, and water. Add plenty of ice, and
fill with orange and lemon slices for a mouth-watering presentation.
Find the link to our cupcake, shortbread cookie, and punch recipes
on our website: HolidayWithMatthewMead.com.

SIMPLY SWEET

Make your own party décor: **1.** Jazz up a cake stand by using double-stick tape to adhere cheery circles made using a Fiskars® punch and gift wrap. **2.** Give guests a small takeaway gift. Find the template for these pretty treat pockets on our website: HolidayWithMatthewMead.com. **3.** Tint shortbread cookie dough with food coloring to match the summery palette. **4.** Embellish glass drink stirrers using paper circles and monogram stickers.

PINK AND YELLOW
For the guest of honor: a wall vase memento to take
home and hang from a doorknob or hook. Fill a
vintage glass bottle with some of the blooms from the
party and tie ribbon around the neck.

Open-air parties in the warmer months provide an abundance of natural, fragrant décor. By taking a celebration outside, you can take advantage of the sweet scent and color of seasonal flowers, the warmth of the sun, and ample entertaining space. Simply haul out a sturdy table, some rustic wooden benches for seating, and plenty of easy-to-make treats. Create oh-so-simple take-away gifts by filling cellophane bags or paper pockets with nuts and chocolate.

"Holding my birthday in such an unexpected location truly caught me off-guard. What an idyllic spot for a birthday celebration!"
— Lisa Renauld

BREEZY STYLE
Pink hydrangea blossoms fill glass cylinders (OPPOSITE). A vintage mattress-ticking tarp (ABOVE), hung using grommets and twine, provides afternoon shade. Make a pennant banner by ironing fusible webbing to fabric. Cut out triangle shapes, punch a hole on each side, and thread with twine.

PUNCH, PAPER, SCISSORS

These projects prove that recycling can be truly stylish. Look through your stash of old gift wrap or craft paper to create simple party décor and take-home favors.

WHAT YOU'LL NEED:

○ Fiskars® circle punch

○ Gift wrap or scrapbook paper

○ Scissors

○ Double-stick tape

○ Pencil and tracing paper

○ Paper pocket template

○ Ribbon

○ Silk flower blossoms

STEP ONE Using a Fiskars® punch and the paper of your choice, cut out enough paper circles to embellish a cake stand and drink stirrers. Apply a piece of double-stick tape to the back of each circle and adhere in an overlapping fashion to the rim of the cake stand.

STEP TWO Place a drink stirrer between two paper circles lined with double-stick tape and press to secure. Personalize each stirrer by adding monogram stickers to one side of the paper circles.

STEP THREE Print the paper pocket template found on our website: HolidayWithMatthewMead.com. Use tracing paper and a pencil to trace the template onto the paper of your choice and cut out using scissors.

STEP FOUR Apply double-stick tape to the edges and fold each side together, tucking in the bottom flap. Press to seal the edges firmly.

STEP FIVE Place a few chocolate treats into each pocket and close the top flap. Wrap ribbon around each pocket and finish with a silk flower blossom secured with tape.

ME AND MY SHADOW

Whether you gather a mismatched collection of interesting objects in a shadow box or use one to unify a specific collection, the simple act of grouping treasured collectibles this way results in an artistic study that honors the significance of each item.

way TO DISPLAY

PLAN THE DISPLAY
Gather your favorite decorative accessories together to create a very personal montage within the frame of a shadow box. Choose from a variety of shadow boxes in different sizes to allow for unlimited display options.

INSIDE THE BOX

The beauty of this type of display is that it isn't permanent and never has to be complete. Objects can be moved around and switched out as you please, and adding seasonal style is as simple as replacing a few of the display pieces or embellishing them with festive flourishes. Using shadow boxes for display is a fun way to change things up. Try different objects in different cubbies, and view your shadow boxes as ever-changing collages that allow you to unleash your creativity.

A SHADOW BOX is to your home what a bulletin board is to your office desk: a way to bring thoughtful organization to the items that you collect. Matthew combs flea markets, thrift stores, and antiques shops for all types of interesting objects (ABOVE) for his home and business. In the process, he not only finds many wonderful pieces to add to his collections, but also interesting items to use as shadow boxes for displaying those finds. An old shipping crate with divided cubbies (OPPOSITE) is refined by adding moldings to its top and bottom to create a sophisticated room-sized shadow box. Within each shelf resides a mix of accessories including handmade baskets, post cards and prints, old thread bobbins, vintage vases, and pedestals made of pottery and alabaster. "The unity here is mostly borne of color and texture," says Matthew. "Each cubby can stand on its own as a study, but together it makes one large impactful and artistic statement. I love how a shadow box brings interest to a room's interior design, while at the same time defining and creating relationships between the things we collect."

I love the cleverness and surprise of using sports memorabilia cases as impromptu glass houses for Jenny's collection of mid-century modern dollhouse furniture.
— Matthew

BLACK AND WHITE

Shadow boxes can be made more interesting by choosing ones that reflect your creativity. Old scale cases (OPPOSITE) become stately display for shapely Bristol glass vases in shades of beige and brown. Stack the cases on a side table and top with an interesting sculpture for a dramatic focal point in a room.

THIS PAGE: **1.** An old aquarium holds vintage urns and a marble bust to create a study with an Eastern sensibility. **2.** A galvanized industrial box pays homage to metropolitan finds including a "city" sign, a memento of the Empire State Building, a flag pole finial, and a numbered mailbox plate. **3.** A large collection is attractive but can be tricky to display. Once grouped in a shadow box setting, however, it becomes purposeful décor that makes a unified statement.

BITS AND BOBS

A vintage, glass lamp base (ABOVE) holds an array of special flatware serving-pieces. A pressed-glass finial offers a pretty, final flourish to the socket fitting. Matthew found cast-off pieces of wooden furniture embellishments (OPPOSITE) in a box at the flea market for twenty dollars. Using wood glue and finishing nails, he added them to a shadow box made from an old silverware drawer-organizer.

TIME PIECE

Take an old clock that is missing its mechanical parts and slip in a favorite old brooch or jewelry pendant for a unique shadow box with time-tested appeal.

WHAT YOU'LL NEED:

- ○ An old clock case/cabinet
- ○ A vintage brooch or jewelry piece
- ○ Handwritten letters or scripted scrapbook paper
- ○ Scissors
- ○ Cardboard
- ○ Double-stick tape
- ○ Hot glue gun

STEP ONE Clean and dust the clock case with a damp cloth and assemble your supplies.

STEP TWO Set the clock case on top of a piece of sturdy cardboard and trace around it using a pencil. Repeat using a piece of scrapbook paper or handwritten letter. Use scissors to cut out the shapes and set aside as backings for the new shadow box.

STEP THREE Using a hot glue gun, add tiny dots of glue to the tips of the brooch and adhere it to the inside of the clock face. Attach pieces of double-stick tape to the back of the scrapbook paper or hand-written letter and, lining it up with the cardboard template, press the paper to secure firmly to the cardboard; smooth out any wrinkles.

STEP FOUR Fit the paper-covered cardboard template into the back of the clock case. Display on a mantel, table, or shelf.

PAINT AND PAPER

Even a novice recycler knows that paint is the modern DIY-er's best friend. But a paint palette boasting glorious color and paired with the prettiest of papers? Well, the results are nothing short of savvy perfection.

DIVINE COLOR
Revive a collection of old bottles with a complementary paint palette; the sheen of the glass intensifies the color. Fill each bottle halfway with paint and swirl it around to coat the interior. Pour out the remaining paint and let dry for 3-5 days; repeat process to ensure even coverage. An old Syroco piece (OPPOSITE) is refreshed with a coat of pink paint.

TIP: If adding fresh flowers to the bottles, be sure to insert the flowers into a water pick first for "paint-free" hydration.

PAPER PARADE

An assortment of floral papers was the inspiration for the décor in this colorful space. A large paper lantern makes a graphic statement (OPPOSITE) and complements the pillows made using vintage fabrics.

Put extra paper to creative use: **1.** Cut strips of scrapbook paper and glue them onto ordinary pencils. **2.** An old dresser is given a coat of fresh coat of paint and inlaid with wallpaper door panels. To recreate, simply use découpage medium to adhere the paper to each door panel. **3.** A piece of leftover wrapping paper is applied to a humble table in need of some TLC. Prepare the surface by painting the table in the desired hue and let dry overnight. Apply a coat of découpage medium to the top of the table and apply the paper; smooth and let dry thoroughly. Seal with a coat of specially-formulated découpage finish (available at art and hobby stores).

STRENGTH IN NUMBERS

Use paint to unify a collection for a curated effect. Syroco pieces, wall plaques, and an old tray are swathed in the same paint color as the wall on which they hang, drawing attention to their carved detailing and charm. OPPOSITE: A flea market tray, lined with a pretty piece of wallpaper, corrals a collection of frames. Use scrapbook papers to dress up worn-out photo frames. Follow the directions on page 84 to repurpose your own.

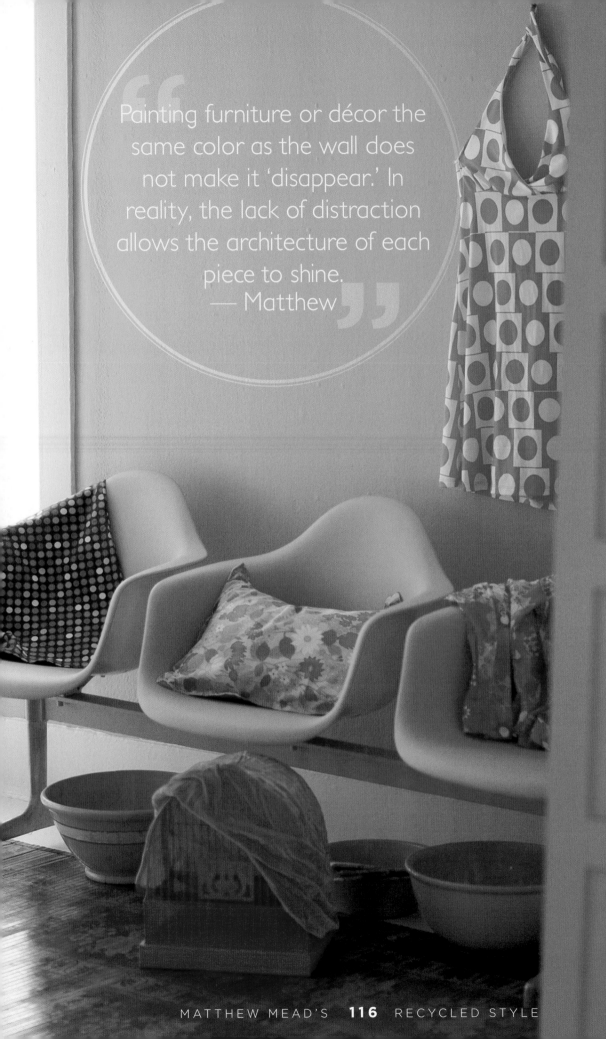

"
Painting furniture or décor the
same color as the wall does
not make it 'disappear.' In
reality, the lack of distraction
allows the architecture of each
piece to shine.
— Matthew
"

SHADES OF GLORY

Swap out an old lampshade with an inexpensive self-adhesive shade covered in gorgeous patterned paper. For less than $25 and an hour of your time, you'll have a lamp worthy of the spotlight.

WHAT YOU'LL NEED:

- Lamp
- Self-adhesive lampshade kit
- Scrapbook paper, gift wrap, or wallpaper
- Scissors
- Pencil
- Ruler

STEP ONE Purchase a self-adhesive lampshade kit (can be found for $10-20 at craft supplies stores like Michaels).

STEP TWO Remove the old lampshade from the lamp. Set aside for use in future lamp refurbishing projects.

STEP THREE Remove cellophane from lampshade kit. Use the paper arc template as a guide and set it on top of your chosen paper.

STEP FOUR Use a pencil to trace around the arc shape and cut out the paper shade. Set arc template aside.

STEP FIVE Carefully attach the paper shade to the sticky surface of the lampshade, lining the edges up as you wrap it around the shade.

STEP SIX Smooth out any wrinkles and attach the shade to the lamp.

Find old lamps in thrift shops and flea markets everywhere. If the wiring is safe, a new or refreshed shade can bring it back to life in an instant.

step-by-step
undercover garden

Terrariums are all the rage these days. Perhaps its because they make gardening effortlessly easy and enjoyable indoors. Whatever your reasons, try one today using this simple plan.

"I like to use flowers to add color to this tabletop focal point, but a mix of green plants is just as pretty."
— Matthew

WHAT YOU'LL NEED:

- ○ Covered glass container
- ○ *Or* a glass jar and separate domed lid
- ○ Small pebbles
- ○ Indoor potting soil
- ○ Plants, foliage, and flowering varieties

STEP ONE It's important to use potting soil labeled for indoor use for this garden. The mix of components and fertilizer are appropriate for the indoor environment, which tends to be drier.

STEP TWO The beauty of a terrarium is that you can use any glass container with a lid. Any size. Any shape. "I've seen gardens so small they fit in a Christmas ornament," Matthew says. "But for this project, I used a modern vase with a large mouth, which makes it easy to insert plants. The lid is actually a glass cheese dome I bought at a flea market for a few dollars."

STEP THREE Place small stones in the bottom of the vessel to collect water. The stones should be about ¼-inch diameter, such as these river pebbles. Array the stones loosely, and make a layer in the bottom that is about a half-inch deep.

STEP FOUR Top the stones with potting soil. The soil will need to be deep enough for the roots, and packed densely enough to support the plant. For most plants you'll need about 2 inches of soil.

STEP FIVE Tuck in your favorite plants. "I used pansies, primrose, and phlox for an array of springtime blooms," Matthew says.

TIP: Terrariums make excellent gifts. Pick a vessel that is unique and personal, then fill it with plants your friend or loved one would enjoy. Attach a pretty tag with care instructions.

STEP SIX "The best part about a terrarium is that it is a mini-ecosystem and is, for the most part, self-watering," Matthew says. To keep the terrarium healthy, remove the glass top once a week for a few hours to let fresh air into the vessel. At this time, mist the plants gently with fresh, room-temperature tap water from a spray bottle. It also helps to aerate (loosen) the soil periodically, which you can do with a table fork.

WHITENING AGENT

Who better than designer Tricia Foley to share her secrets for using—and reusing—furniture and accessories? In her ultra-light house, she focuses on the outward beauty and inherent utility of each item, regardless of whether it's a valuable flea-market find or an inexpensive purchase from a big box store. Let her wisdom guide practices in your home.

CHARM SCHOOL
The clawfoot tub was the only fixture Tricia saved when she bought the house. Her father brought her the salvaged porcelain sink during the renovation period, when Tricia was stripping away previous remodeling work that was unsafe and unflattering to restore original character. "He said, 'This looks like you, this piece of junk,' the way only fathers can," she says with a laugh.

REINVENTION IS A CONSTANT STATE in Tricia Foley's Long Island home. The stylist, designer, author, and, now, entrepreneur, evolves with new interests—and her house does, too. Her collections are always on display and in use, her furniture resting between moves to different rooms. "Everything here has to work hard to earn its keep," she says, with a laugh. This philosophy is not a joke, however. At her three-times-a-year occasional sales called The New General Store, Tricia is likely to sell off a platter, vase, or sideboard that is no longer serving a function in her home. "I really do use things," she says. "Some collectors look for more unusual, decorative, or unique stuff. I like useful things." An item proves its worth when Tricia can employ it for entertaining as well as everyday living, during one season or another, indoors or out. She pulls a shallow concrete planter off her patio to hold summery seashells on the living room coffee table, for example. A plate rack in her dining room has graced other homes and other rooms. "It has been a few different colors," she says. "I have a huge collection of china, which I use for entertaining, as containers for storage, or for display." To earn Tricia's loyalty, a piece has to be versatile. And that goes for her refurbished 1820s house in Yaphank, New York. White walls, dark floors, and plenty of simply dressed windows make it a neutral, accepting backdrop for whatever Tricia has planned for the day, which may be a magazine photo shoot, research for product design, or a dinner party for friends involved in her sales. "I see the house as a consistent palette, but I use different textures and objects to change it up," she says.

RECYCLING EFFORTS

It was a balancing act to bring her older home up to modern day standards while still preserving the charm that drew her to the house in the first place, Tricia says. She reuses old bottles as vases (ABOVE, LEFT), or to hold cooking oils or bath salts. Tricia found many of the home's original doors in the garage and added "new" vintage hardware she picked up at flea markets (ABOVE, RIGHT).

LIVING ARRANGEMENTS

A combination of two small spaces, the living room functions well as a dining area when Tricia moves in a long table for gatherings of her big extended family. Glossy white paint on the 8-foot-tall ceilings bounces light into the room. One of five in the house, the sitting room fireplace (OPPOSITE) is often put to use on chilly nights. Tricia arrays a collection of glass vessels as objets d'art. She chooses interesting shapes, then staggers them according to height and mixes translucent and opaque ones evenly.

"I think of all those matched-set, polyester sheets in sale catalogs and shiver. These soft vintage textiles are very comforting."
— Tricia Foley

BEDTIME STORIES

Tricia has always been a flea market shopper for sheets and pillowcases (OPPOSITE) that are supple with age and wear. "I used to look for linens that were the prettiest and most embroidered," Tricia says. "Now I look for things that stand up to wear and have simple details." She mixes up the different shades—white, cream, and tan—deliberately. "It's more interesting, more visually appealing," she says. Propping a round mirror on the bedroom mantel turns it into a casual vanity if needed. The very dark accents Tricia sprinkles sparingly throughout the house act like design exclamation points.

TRICKS FOR BRIGHTER WHITES

Tricia's tricks for getting brighter linens, glassware, and ceramics aren't tricks at all—they are time-tested remedies that may be as close as your pantry.

WHAT YOU'LL NEED:

- Comet® cleanser
- White vinegar
- Ammonia
- Newspaper
- Lemons
- Ivory Soap Flakes
- Sunshine
- Bleach

CHINA "Being a tea lover and white cup collector, I inevitably have tea-stained cups and teapots," says designer Tricia Foley. To banish the brown, she soaks the ceramic pieces in a gallon of warm water with a ¼-cup of Comet® cleaner dissolved in it. "That does the trick, and then you just need to wipe them out and wash normally."

GLASSWARE To refresh a glass that has become cloudy, fill it with white vinegar and let soak. Rinse and repeat as needed. To make windows sparkle, Tricia says nothing beats the age-old ammonia solution: Fill a 1-gallon bucket with warm water and add ½-cup of ammonia. Wash the windows with a soft cloth dipped in the solution. Dry with crumpled pieces of newspaper "for a clean finish," she says.

TABLE LINENS For recent stains: "I treat tea or coffee stains right away with just a squeeze of juice from half a lemon, with a pad of paper towels under the cloth for absorption," Tricia says. For vintage tea towels, tablecloths, and napkins that are dingy or gray with age, Tricia washes them using Ivory® dish liquid. If more treatment is needed, boil them in a big lobster or pasta pot with a basic powdered detergent like Tide®. "Soak them, stir them, swirl the fabric around, and repeat a few times to freshen the water," she says. "Then I drape them on my porch railing to let the sun whiten them."

BED LINENS AND BATH TOWELS A ¼-cup of liquid bleach is often all that's needed to brighten a load of whites. "If possible, hang them to dry them on a clothesline," Tricia says. "It keeps them whiter and the natural fresh-air fragrance can't be beat!"

SLIPCOVERS "White canvas slipcovers are my go-to solution for bringing old chairs and sofas back to life," Tricia says. To keep them bright, she launders them with a bit of bleach ("but not too much and don't let them soak too long," she advises). She puts them back on before they are completely dry. "They will be more supple to put on, and will dry without too many wrinkles," she says.

TIP: To keep these ingredients and methods handy, cut out the pages and tape them to your laundry wall, take a snapshot of the pages with your phone, or download the tips from HolidayWithMatthewMead.com.

step-by-step
waxing
nostalgic

Known for her elegant way with repurposed objects, Lee Repetto of The Spotted Cod shop in Sandwich, Massachusetts, shows us how to turn a flea market find into a valuable decorative asset.

"This table cost only $20, and it was pretty mundane. But with Lee's touch, it looks like an expensive designer find."
— Matthew

WHAT YOU'LL NEED:

- ○ #000 Extra-fine steel wool
- ○ Painter's or masking tape
- ○ Tack Cloth
- ○ Latex Paint
- ○ Acrylic crafts paint
- ○ Paintbrush
- ○ Briwax®
- ○ Soft, clean dry rags

STEP ONE Before she started treating the table, Lee taped off the decorative brass fittings, including medallions on the legs, brackets at the corners, and cuffs above the feet. Any masking tape will work, she says, but blue painter's tape comes in a variety of widths, so she was able to cover the brass cuffs completely with one band of 2-inch-wide tape.

STEP TWO Lee covered other fittings on the table, as well. Sometimes, Lee says, it's easier to take a piece of furniture apart to separate the wood pieces and the hardware. But that would have been too time-consuming and difficult with this table, which had several glued-together joints. She didn't want to risk disturbing the glue, which dates back to when the piece was made, probably in the early 1980s.

STEP THREE To ready the piece for paint, Lee first roughed up the finish on the maple wood using fine steel wool. This takes the shine off the finish, so the new paint will adhere well. Then she went over each surface and into the nooks, crannies, and corners with tack cloth, a slightly sticky piece of cheesecloth that picks up the dust from sanding.

TIP: To reuse leftover paint for craft projects, seal the lid tightly after each use. An open can of latex paint will last up to two years. If it has separated, stir it vigorously or take it to the paint store to have it shaken until the ingredients mix smoothly together again.

STEP FOUR Lee chose a favorite shade of blue-green called "Arsenic" by Farrow & Ball. She had some leftover from another project. But rather than paint the table with a coat of flat color, Lee stirred in a few squirts of a sage green crafts paint she had on hand. The latex and acrylic paints don't mix evenly together, which gave Lee the striations in color she desired.

STEP FIVE To create a patina of texture and age for the table, Lee used two colors of paint stirred together, and applied the mixture with a small brush, deliberately trying to achieve brushstrokes. She painted the piece three times, applying a thin coat of color each time, and letting each layer dry completely.

STEP SIX Finally, using a clean wad of extra-fine steel wool, Lee knocked the sheen off the new paint finish, and even rubbed through to bare wood in a few places, mimicking the wear and tear of time. Sandpaper is too harsh for this delicate work, she says. She prefers steel wool, even though it can be time consuming to go over the surface repeatedly. The result, however, is velvety to the touch.

STEP SEVEN At this point in the process, most people apply a coat of clear polyurethane sealant to protect the paint finish. But Lee prefers the look and feel of a coat of wax, a time-honored way to seal furniture. She uses Briwax®, an English import. Using a dry rag, she rubbed wax on the table's surfaces, working it into the grain. The pigment in the wax settles into the grain's texture, creating interesting highlights and lowlights in the finish. With another clean, dry rag, she removed some of the wax and buffed the surface to a satiny shine.

STEP EIGHT Many times, tray tables like this one are intended to be used as portable bars. However, this version is short, making it a little too low for comfortable drink-mixing. Instead, Lee uses it as a nightstand or sofa table.

DESIGN ON A DIME

Achieve the style you love without breaking the bank: Head to the thrift shop in search of sturdy, cast-off furniture with classic silhouettes and use paint and fabric to give them modern flair.

SWEET SALVATION

Shop local thrift stores like the Salvation Army and the Goodwill for rock-bottom prices on home furnishings. For $200 we found the side chair, sofa, metal box, china cabinet, and lamp base to fill this room (BELOW). To revive the sofa, we painted its frame gray, applied a medium-brown glaze over top, and then had it re-upholstered in an affordable linen fabric.

STENCIL AWAY
Ivory colored pillows go from drab to fab
using just a stencil and fabric paint to create
a custom design. See directions on page 152.

A galvanized storage box becomes a unique conversation piece when used as a coffee table. With the addition of locking wheels, it can be easily moved.

IN TOP FORM
A tired, outdated china cabinet makes a bold style statement when recast in a colorful finish. See directions on page 148.

BUTTONED UP
We made a stylish lamp by inserting a sheet of ombré-patterned paper, in shades of blue, into an inverted glass cylinder. Vintage buttons in coordinating colors are glued along the lamp's shade.

MODERN PEDIGREE

An old china cabinet, with exquisite detailing but a rough finish, required little more than some paint and mat board to highlight its fine form.

WHAT YOU'LL NEED:

○ Tack cloth

○ Paint brushes

○ Screwdriver

○ Hammer

○ Zinsser™ Bulls-Eye 1-2-3 primer

○ California Paint's DE 5779 Bayshore

○ Gray mat board (cut to size at a frame shop)

STEP ONE Clean and dust all surfaces of the cabinet to prepare it for priming.

STEP TWO To give this distinctly 1950's Colonial Revival china cabinet an updated, modern feel—and better highlight the inlaid design of the doors—we removed the top cornice piece using a screwdriver and hammer. Set aside for use in other furniture repurposing projects.

STEP THREE Carefully remove the old glass and inlaid wooden frame from each cabinet door. Set aside the glass fasteners to use when inserting the mat board into each door frame.

STEP FOUR Remove the door knobs and drawer pulls before priming and painting. Apply one coat of Zinsser™ Bulls-Eye 1-2-3 primer and let fully dry. Follow up with two coats of satin-finish latex paint in your desired color (we used paint color DE 5779 Bayshore).

STEP FIVE Install the mat board into each inlaid frame and insert into the door frames; secure using the original glass fasteners. Reinstall the door knobs and drawer pulls to finish.

TABLE TO GO

Create a moveable coffee/storage table using a large cast-off tool box, four lockable wheels, and some metal epoxy.

WHAT YOU'LL NEED:

- Large galvanized-metal storage box
- J-B Weld® epoxy
- Four lockable wheels (from the hardware store or Home Depot)
- Ruler and pencil
- Small paint brush
- Rag

STEP ONE Invert the metal storage box to attach the wheels. Use a ruler to mark where the wheels should go and follow the directions on the epoxy tube to adhere the wheels to each corner. Wipe away any excess epoxy using a rag and avoid getting epoxy on your fingers.

STEP TWO Allow epoxy to set, following the manufacturer's instructions. Once completely dry, turn the table over and lock the wheels in place for use as a coffee table.

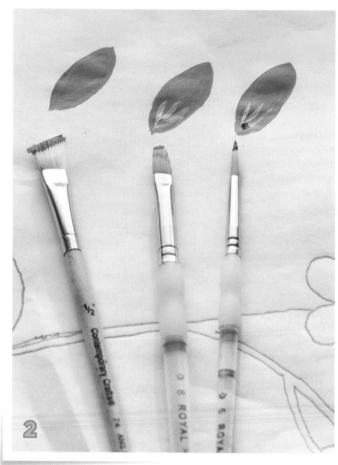

FLOWER POWER

Customize plain-Jane cast-off pillows with a simple-to-make template and some craft paint. Practice your paint strokes on paper first, and you'll be on your way to creating your own personal painterly style.

WHAT YOU'LL NEED:

- White printer paper
- Fine-point scissors
- Pencil, not sharp
- 16 x 16-inch piece of cardboard
- Floral stencil template (download at HolidayWithMatthewMead.com)
- Plain cotton, linen, or canvas pillows

- Acrylic fabric paint in desired hues (We used several shades of blue for the flowers and a light gray for the background paint wash.)
- A 1½-inch chip brush and acrylic paint brushes: white nylon ½-inch angular flat brush, a filbert #8, a round #5

STEP ONE Remove the pillow insert from the pillow case. Insert a flat sheet of cardboard. Place pillow on clean, flat, paper-covered surface. Place a dab of gray paint in a small porcelain dish. Add drops of water until paint is thinned, like a liquid. Use the chip brush and neutral-colored paint (we used gray) to wash the pillow with a paint wash, using feather-light strokes. Let dry thoroughly. Print and cut out the stencil using fine-tip scissors. Place the stencil on the fabric in the desired place and trace a light design using a pencil.

STEP TWO Begin by dipping the angular flat brush in the mid-tone paint and fill in the almond-shaped petal tracings. Let dry. Next, use the filbert brush in a contrasting color to create highlights on the base of the petal; let dry. Use the round brush in the darkest shade of paint to create a final dot detail at the base of the leaf.

STEP THREE Branch out the design by using contrasting colors for each of the petals. Repeat the directions in step two to create color variation in your tracing design. To create the dots on the center of the flower, dip the handle end of the paint brush into a small amount of paint at a 90 degree angle and dab it onto the fabric in a quick motion.

STEP FOUR Allow each pillow to dry overnight and spot clean as needed; avoid laundering in a washing machine.

TIP: Make your own stencils using copy-right free Dover books. Simply photocopy the images and use tracing paper to transfer the images onto craft paper. Find a library of images and designs at DoverPublications.com.

SHADES OF OMBRÉ

Fashion a new lamp out of some old parts, including a collection of mismatched buttons, a glass cylinder jar, and a discarded lamp shade.

WHAT YOU'LL NEED:

- ○ Ombré-patterned paper template (download at HolidayWithMatthewMead.com)
- ○ Glass cylinder jar
- ○ Lamp kit from Lampshop.com
- ○ Clear epoxy for glass
- ○ Scissors
- ○ Plain lamp shade
- ○ Glue gun and hot glue
- ○ Vintage buttons in shades of blue

STEP ONE Measure the circumference and depth of your jar and cut the ombré paper template to fit. Bring each end of the paper together and secure on the inside edge using tape; insert the patterned paper into the glass jar.

STEP TWO Invert the jar and, following the manufacturer's lamp kit directions, use the clear epoxy to adhere the lamp fittings to the top of the lamp base, as shown. (The lamp cord is attached to the neck of the lamp, so no drilling is required for this project.)

1   2

STEP THREE Use hot glue to attach the buttons along the circumference of the lamp shade, lining them up along the center.

STEP FOUR Attach the lamp shade to the lamp's base. Swap out the paper in the base of the lamp seasonally, or just for a change in aesthetic.

BERRIES, CHERRIES, AND BAKEWARE

Vintage bakeware is not only useful and easy to find, but each piece is a tried and true ingredient for old-fashioned baking. We rounded up our collection—and an assortment of nature's candy—to uncover the many uses of these "well-seasoned" pans.

A DIME A DOZEN
Strawberries are even sweeter when served in a heart-shaped cake pan (OPPOSITE). Purchase old baking tins for a song at yard sales, flea markets and thrift stores. Repurpose them to serve food, display flowers, or to decorate a kitchen wall.

WHAT COULD BE MORE WHOLESOME than baking up old-fashioned recipes in humble bakeware that has stood the test of time? Known for their graphic shapes and fluting, this hard-working bakeware boasts an aged patina that takes us back to the simplicity and nostalgia of the past—when we watched our grandmothers carefully line pie tins with their sure-to-be-flaky crust or fill a cake pan with sweet batter. While we happily licked the beaters, the tantalizing scent of baked goods filled the kitchen.

FILLED WITH SWEETNESS
A vintage madeleine pan (OPPOSITE) is perfect for serving a mix of fresh preserves to spread atop thin slices of toasted oatmeal bread. Fill the molds with a handful of fresh berries and a dollop each of strawberry, blueberry, and cherry preserves. ABOVE: Bring vintage baking tins out into the field and fill them with berries. Serve immediately for a true farm-to-table experience. Miniature bread pans hold a pint-sized measure of fresh strawberries for seasonal gifts; attach a note card with a favorite recipe.

GRAND STAND

Make a tiered serving stand (OPPOSITE) using a few lamp parts and some paint, and serve a mix of fresh berries to top yogurt, ice cream or cake. A square and round cake pan can be stacked to create a cherry shortcake serving station (BELOW). Repurpose a single candlestick as a riser and use epoxy to adhere it to the top and bottom of the stand. Fill with homemade biscuits, Bing cherries, and a side of cream.

SWEET APPEAL
Fluted tins produce the prettiest tart shells. Prepare simple strawberry tarts (ABOVE) by placing two berries in each baked shell and top them with a drizzle of strawberry sauce. Put a fresh spin on a shortcake dessert by using fresh cherries. Serve cherry shortcakes—layered with the sweet fruit and a generous serving of whipped cream—in vintage enamelware pie plates (OPPOSITE) for old-fashioned charm. Sprinkle the top of each dessert with poppy seeds and finish with a cherry on top. Find all recipes on page 254 and at HolidayWithMatthewMead.com.

BERRY BLISS

Summer is the perfect time to find fresh berries and vintage bakeware. Farm stands and flea markets are in full bloom, offering the elements needed to create these delicious desserts. Strawberry cake (ABOVE) is spread with a layer of cream cheese and topped with fresh strawberry sauce. Blueberry shortcake bars (OPPOSITE) combine the goodness of shortbread with homemade blueberry pie filling. Find all recipes on page 254 and at HolidayWithMatthewMead.com.

BAKE STAND

Repurpose some vintage bakeware into a spiffy tiered stand using a few simple supplies.
Fill each tier with baked goods or fresh fruit for use as a striking summer centerpiece.

WHAT YOU'LL NEED:

- Tiered-stand conversion kit from Lampshop.com

- One 8-inch and one 9¾-inch vintage pie plate

- Awl and hammer

- Black pen or marker

- Black and gray acrylic craft paint

- Small paintbrush

- Thick slab of Styrofoam™

STEP ONE Blend a small amount of black and gray paint together and apply lightly to the metal conversion pieces, until their patina mimics that of the pie plates. Let dry and apply second coat.

STEP TWO Place one of the pie plates on top of the Styrofoam™ slab. Use a pen to mark the center of the pie plate. Center the awl on the mark and use a hammer to bang the point of the awl through the pie plate, creating a hole.

STEP THREE Repeat step two using the second pie plate.

STEP FOUR Thread the conversion kit through the pie plates (using the 8-inch pie plate for the top tier), and secure the bottom plate with the provided bolt and washer; finish with the finial end for the top of the stand.

STEP FIVE Fill each tier with fruit, tarts, or your favorite seasonal décor.

PUSHING BUTTONS

Free on shirt hems, sold by the jarful at flea markets, buttons are as common as pennies—and as lucky, too, because they are decorative treasures that can inspire a project from the start or finish it with aplomb.

BUTTON ART
Create an inexpensive visual display (OPPOSITE) using a vintage portrait frame, uncut mat board from the crafts store, and hot glue. Select buttons of a theme (these are all made of vegetable ivory), and array different shape, sizes, textures, and hues together. Or, trim the edge of a ho-hum shelf with buttons that are slightly larger than the edge of the board (THIS PAGE).

LITTLE BUTTONS CAN BE A BIG DEAL. Collectors pursue rare gems; societies share favorite finds; museums mount international exhibitions. But the delightful thing about buttons is that they can also be small and intimate and as personal as sifting through Grandma's button box.

Most people amass buttons one or two at a time when they purchase a new garment, and attached to the tag is a small plastic bag containing spare buttons. However, you can also pick them up by the jarful or bagful at estate sales, garage sales, thrift stores, and flea markets. Once upon a time, everyone kept a stash of buttons, either for utilitarian purposes to mend a shirt or sew a dress, or for the pleasure of collecting them.

You may never find a valuable button—at least as far as the National Button Society would define it—but you will find all histories and decorative eras represented, from Victorian to Art Deco. Though the oldest button discovered is about 5,000 years old, the majority of easy-to-find vintage buttons date between the mid-1800s and the early-1900s. You'll find plain ones and ornate ones, large and miniscule buttons, those with carved patterns, some pressed with rhinestones, and buttons in every color of the rainbow. Some of the buttons on these pages are made from vegetable ivory, which was actually the nut of a palm tree. Some are celluloid and Bakelite, which were precursors to plastic. You may also find translucent glass and Lucite buttons, metal ones, and fabric-covered fobs. The variety is what makes them so interesting. "They started out with the utilitarian purpose of fastening clothes," Matthew says. "But the shapes, sizes, and graphic designs make them small works of art."

EASY PICKIN'
Fill a shallow dish or bowl with
particularly textural or eye-catching
buttons, and let your guests pick
through them or scoop up handfuls.

BUTTONS ON DISPLAY

Give plain woven baskets elegant embellishment (OPPOSITE). First, spray-paint the basket in a hue that complements the button you've chosen. Then rub the baskets with wax (we used BriWax® in Light Brown) to give them an aged patina akin to the buttons. Finally, hot-glue a button to the front, and hot-glue a loop of elastic-string to the underside of the lid for the closure. **1.** Factories used these shallow wooden trays in the making of buttons. Use them to display your collection. **2.** Paint in earthy shades, such as loden green and charcoal gray, show off the creamy hues of vegetable-ivory buttons. **3.** These buttons are still attached to their card, likely part of a wholesaler's display or a general store's offerings. Look for finds like this at flea markets.

CUTE AS A...

Try one of these quick ideas: **1.** Nestle a votive inside a large glass or jar, and fill the gap with buttons. **2.** Use buttons to trim a picture frame. **3.** Sew them onto the corners of cocktail napkins. **4.** Make bottle sleeves out of kraft paper, and glue on the button medallions.

SEW EASY

Fashion this quick pick-me-up for any upholstered ottoman, bench, chair, or pillow. Tack buttons to #40 wide satin ribbon using needle and thread, then wrap the ribbon around the piece. For a temporary look, pin the ribbon in place with upholstery pins, or use fabric glue to securely attach it.

MEMO BOARD

Keep notes and mementoes at hand with this stylish organizer.

WHAT YOU'LL NEED:

- 24 x 18-inch piece of cork
- 1 yard of fabric
- Ribbons in several widths
- Upholstery tacks
- Hot glue gun
- Stapler

STEP ONE Measure and cut a 28x22-inch piece of fabric. This velvet provides a rich look.

STEP TWO Smooth the fabric across the front of the corkboard and wrap the edges around to the backside. Flip board over and secure the edges at even intervals with upholstery tacks.

STEP THREE Cut ribbon pieces to cover the width of the cork board and wrap 2 inches to the back. Tack to secure.

STEP FOUR Hot-glue buttons to the heads of brass upholstery tacks. When dry, use takes to pin notes, photos, and reminders to the board.

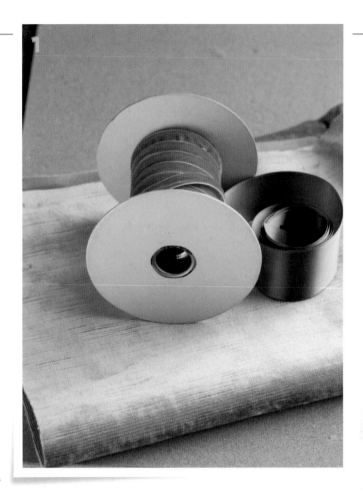

TABLE LAMP

Whether you fix up a flea market find, or customize a store-bought lamp to suit your décor, buttons are the answer.

WHAT YOU'LL NEED:

- ○ Lamp base
- ○ Plain shade
- ○ Acrylic craft paint
- ○ Water
- ○ Paper towels
- ○ Hot-glue gun

STEP ONE To stir up a soft wash of color that will perk up this outdated lamp base, combine paint and water in a 2:1 ratio in a bowl.

STEP TWO Brush on the paint mixture. Use a damp paper towel to rub off extra paint. Let dry.

STEP THREE Hot-glue buttons around the lampshade using a ruler, popsicle stick, or another spacer to ensure equal spacing between buttons. To make a level border, place the center of the button 1 inch from the bottom edge of the shade. (If the buttons are larger than 1 inch diameter, increase this distance accordingly.) Stick a piece of painter's tape to mark the line on the inside of the shade, and use it to guide placement of the buttons. When finished, remove the tape.

MORE ABOUT BUTTONS

There's so much more to know about these fashionable fobs. Check out these books, societies, and online sources for collecting information, cleaning tips, and project ideas:

CREATE:
Button Ware by Amy Barickman
Button It Up by Susan Beal

READ:
The Collector's Encyclopedia of Buttons by Sally C. Luscomb
Button Button: Identification and Price Guide by Peggy Ann Osborne

SEARCH:
Vintage Button Guide by Jamie Brock (JamieBrock.hubpages.com)
"Button Crafts" on Pinterest.com

JOIN:
A local club of the National Button Society
(NationalButtonSociety.org)

BY THE SEA

Look no further than the sea to find all you need for easy summer entertaining and decorating ideas. An afternoon spent exploring the shoreline can yield a bounty of ocean treasures that can be incorporated into beach-inspired summer projects.

WHAT BETTER WAY TO ENJOY SUMMER than to take in the sights, smells, and sounds of our ocean playgrounds? Most of us can recall, with joy, our first childhood trip to the beach. As the sand squished between our toes, we filled our pails with shiny stones, shells, and beach glass, all while scanning for the elusive sand dollar. Once home, we admired our finds and kept them "just because," as happy reminders of a fun-filled day at the beach. Bring back that foraging spirit and head to the seaside to line your pockets and pails with all you need to inject coastal style into your home. An afternoon spent beach-combing can provide a treasure-trove of materials to put to use when dressing up your summer tablescapes and lining your own grown-up shelves with ocean-inspired décor and memorabilia.

COASTAL COLLECTIONS
A salvaged wire basket (OPPOSITE) displays just some of the shells found during a summer's worth of treasure-seeking.
(ABOVE LEFT): Who hasn't put a shell to their ear to hear the sound of the ocean calling? A 1970's curio shelf (ABOVE RIGHT) goes coastal with a fresh coat of white paint and some glued-on seashells and beach stones.

Make a summer afternoon date with your glue gun, a bag of seashells, and some foam balls. Make one ball a week and by summer's end, a collection will be born.

SEA AND DO

A recycled metal tray holds the bounty from a summer's worth of collecting stones and tiny seashells that can be transformed into beach-inspired summer décor. Use shells to create summer mobiles or a beach-stone garland (ABOVE), created by drilling holes in each stone and threading with jute to hang.

HUNT AND GATHER

Grab your pail and shovel and dig up ocean treasures that can later become embellishments for pretty summer projects. **1.** Each year, choose an item to hunt for on your trips to the beach. Heart-shaped rocks are a sentimental find that can be grouped together in a jar or given as tokens of affection to those you hold dear. **2.** A salvaged metal carburetor is given a wash of white paint and used as a sleeve for a votive candle. Use a saucer or small plate beneath the candle to prevent wax drippings from damaging the tablecloth. **3.** Fill a collection of vintage bamboo flatware in a recycled garden pot and scatter some shells around its base. Later, use the pot to host new beach finds from each trip.

SHELLED OUT

Repurpose a tired or unattractive picture frame by hot-gluing small shells over its front. First, paint the frame with white paint and dab hot glue onto the frame to adhere each shell. When finished, slip in a seashell print or gift card behind the glass for a photo finish. Larger shells may be used to embellish a mirror or over-sized frame.

Heading to the beach is a highlight of my summer weekends. **Nothing beats walking the shoreline**—scanning for shells or bits of beach glass—and then heading home sandy, relaxed, and inspired to use my ocean treasures for simple, summer projects.
— Matthew

SEASIDE SERVICE
Make summery drink stirrers by using hot-glue to attach scallop shells to the ends of bamboo skewers.

SEASIDE SERVICE
We used hot glue to attach seashells to the top of a wire food tent – designed to keep pesky insects away from a tempting stack of profiteroles. Place the skewers in drinks or use them to pierce grapes.

SHELL BY SHELL

Fire up your glue gun to make a variety of projects using seashells and beach finds. Look for a small glue gun which is readily portable, heats up quickly, and has a fine tip to leave little glue residue on your inspired summer décor.

WHAT YOU'LL NEED:

- Paper gift bag
- Seashells
- Glue gun
- Glue sticks
- Styrofoam™ ball

STEP ONE Insert a glue stick into the glue gun and heat it to its maximum temperature.

STEP TWO To create the seashell bag, use a pencil to create a design on the bag before gluing on the shells. Apply a sparing amount of glue to the back of each shell; follow the design to place the shells on the bag and hold them in place until securely adhered.

STEP THREE To create the seashell-studded ball, gather a selection of scallop-shaped shells. Place glue onto the ball and place the seashells on top of the glue. Hold the shells in place until secure. Cover the entire ball and keep shells organized in one direction for the most graphic effect.

FINISHING TOUCHES

Salvaged vintage furniture, with its graceful lines and hardworking history, receives a stylish reinvention with some fresh coats of paint, new hardware, and colorful fabric.

Thrift shops and flea markets are brimming with furniture that has lost some of its beauty. Always prime old furniture before painting to promote durability and to ensure even coverage. Matthew swears by Zinsser™ Bulls-Eye 1-2-3 for one-coat coverage, even without sanding.

TO PAINT OR NOT TO PAINT, that is the oft-asked question. Wood enthusiasts caution against it. "White-washers" do it to everything. Others hem and haw and live with pieces they don't love, simply because they're not sure which camp they belong to. But when you cull your furniture from a secondhand shop, the stakes are a little lower—allowing even the most hesitant decorator to take the plunge. "When a piece of furniture just looks tired and unloved, a coat of paint is often the exact medicine to bring it back to life," Matthew says. "It's only paint!" But he does offer a piece of advice when selecting paint colors: Draw inspiration from what you love. "Glean color palettes from your favorite collectibles and bring them to the paint store for exact matching," suggests Matthew. "Then you can't go wrong!"

THE SMALL STUFF

Poke around the recesses of a thrift shop for smaller items to revive with paint. Old picture frames, not-so-attractive lamps, and small stools (OPPOSITE) are often passed over in favor of more pristine finds. With just some fresh paint and new fabric, they can become treasured décor.

TIP: Refresh old chairs with a matching paint treatment and take comfort a step further by replacing the foam on each seat. An upholsterer will help you select the right foam and fabric to update the chairs. Matthew selected a heavyweight linen fabric in a pale golden hue.

A PERFECT SET

Mismatched table and chairs become one classic set (OPPOSITE), thanks to a unifying paint treatment using some of Matthew's favorite colors. After priming the pieces, Matthew applied Pittsburgh® Paints Manor Hall Stonington in a semi-gloss latex finish. When that layer dried, he painted on the company's complementary hue: Gray-Beige. Matthew then lightly sanded the pieces to reveal some of the under-layer. A thin coat of Minwax® Paste Finishing Wax in Natural gives them lustre and a protective finish.

Sometimes the best makeovers are the most subtle. Reupholstered in an elegant but serviceable linen fabric, the lighter, updated shade showcases the sofa's intricate details.

DUAL FUNCTION

Fabric-covered ottomans serve two purposes: they offer up a place to rest your tired legs at the end of a long day, and can be called into play as a casual coffee table. Simply use a tray to set drinks or small pots of flowers on (ABOVE), and use your vacuum to clean the surface weekly. Prolong the life of the fabric cushion by draping it in a pretty throw, perfect for chillier evenings.

"Don't be afraid to paint cast-off furniture.
It's often the perfect way to bring new
perspective to down-on-their-luck pieces."
— Matthew

PERIOD REVIVAL

Give a reproduction writing desk a face-lift with a coat of Pratt & Lambert's Moss Lake: **1.** When the base coat dries, wash over it with white primer (thinned with equal parts water and then rubbed off with a clean rag) to create an aged effect. **2.** Using leftover fabric from a re-upholstered chair (OPPOSITE), cover the top of the writing desk. Measure the fabric to fit and spread the fabric across the top of the desk and adhere it with spray adhesive. A band of upholstery tacks around the edge secures the fabric and gives the piece new distinction. **3.** A once unattractive lamp fits right in with the new décor after receiving a coat of beige paint and a new linen shade.

MIRROR, MIRROR, ON THE WALL
A tired old picture frame is hung with distinction after receiving a coat of gray paint. Backed with a gray mat board, it becomes the perfect backdrop for a vintage looking glass found at a flea market, allowing the unique mirror to stand out, despite its diminutive size.

FROM BED TO CHAIR

Look for an antique bedstead at an auction and repurpose it into an upright bench. Fill nail holes, sand, and remove dust with a tack cloth before priming and painting. Matthew covered the bench in Pratt & Lambert's Maitland Blue paint, and then using a small brush, hand-painted a dark-gray shadow line to highlight the lines of the bench. Finally, he applied Pratt & Lambert's Ovation glaze in Touch of Mink for a distressed finish.

LIGHTEN UP

This simple lamp project is the perfect example of when it is not only okay to paint over old wood, but truly justified.

WHAT YOU'LL NEED:

- ○ Molded composite or wooden lamp
- ○ Linen shade
- ○ Zinsser™ Bulls-Eye 1-2-3 primer
- ○ Paint brush
- ○ Spray paint (we used Krylon Fusion For Plastic®)

STEP ONE Dust off lamp base with a damp rag and let dry. Cover with one coat of Zinsser™ primer and let dry according to manufacturer's directions on paint can.

STEP TWO Cover electrical cord with painter's tape to protect it from overspray. In a well-ventilated area, apply a light even coat to the lamp base. Let dry fully and reapply until even coverage is achieved. Allow to cure fully before setting on a table surface. Top the lamp base with a matching linen shade.

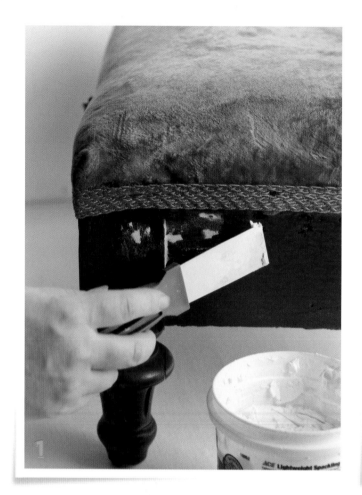

EASY OTTOMAN

Apply new paint and fabric to a worn-out stool or ottoman and then put your feet up and reap the benefit of your efforts.

WHAT YOU'LL NEED:

- ◯ Salvaged stool or ottoman
- ◯ Interior-grade wood filler
- ◯ Putty knife
- ◯ Zinsser™ Bulls-Eye 1-2-3 primer
- ◯ Paint brush
- ◯ Acrylic latex paint
- ◯ Upholstery webbing
- ◯ Staple gun and staples
- ◯ 4-inch upholstery foam
- ◯ Fabric

STEP ONE Prepare the stool or ottoman by repairing any holes or nicks in the wood with wood filler. Sand the repaired areas smooth and wipe dust away with a tack cloth. Remove the foam and upholstery from the stool's surface and discard.

STEP TWO Cover the wooden frame with a coat of Zinsser™ Bulls-Eye 1-2-3 primer. Let dry fully.

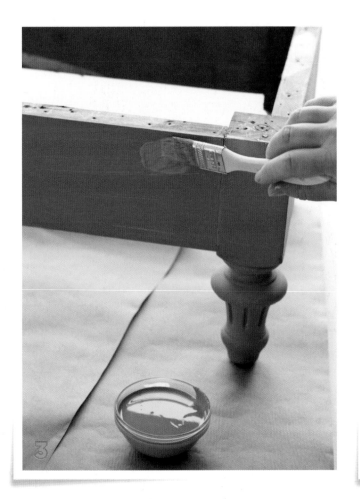

STEP THREE Cover the frame in two to three coats of beige paint and let dry between coats.

STEP FOUR Cut strips of upholstery webbing to match the length and width of the ottoman base. Use a staple gun to attach the strips along two sides of the base. Weave the strips together, pulling taut at the opposite sides and securing with staples.

STEP FIVE Bring the stool to your local upholstery shop where they can secure and wrap the foam with your desired fabric for a reasonable fee.

FRAME IT

Frames needn't be just for paintings and photographs. Fit with mat board to show off other items like mirrors or architectural medallions.

WHAT YOU'LL NEED:

- O Large picture frame
- O Smaller mirror, medallion, or decorative object.
- O Zinsser™ Bulls-Eye 1-2-3 primer
- O Paint brush
- O Acrylic latex paint
- O Gray mat board
- O Letter decals

STEP ONE Coat the picture frame with Zinsser™ Bulls-Eye 1-2-3 primer. Let dry.

STEP TWO Cover the frame in two coats of latex paint (we chose a shade of gray-beige, leaving the inner frame edging white for added interest). Let dry overnight. Purchase a piece of gray mat board and have it custom cut to fit the frame. Pick a spot in the lower third of the mat board to apply decal letters for Roman numerals. Flip the frame over and set the piece of mat board into the back of the frame.

STEP THREE Turn over and hang the frame on the wall using a nail. Hang a smaller mirror or medallion centered above the Roman numerals using a small decorative nail or brad, ensuring the nail goes through the mat board and into the wall for security.

MDCCXVI

CAMPING CHIC

Defy the notion that "roughing it" has to be synonymous with camping. Earn your back-to-nature stripes while indulging in a few of life's luxuries and set the scene with some recycled finds that combine comfort and function with pretty.

TABLE FOR TWO
A vintage wooden table and fold-up chairs are revived with a wash of paint and some recycled floral fabric scraps tied onto the chair backs. Fern fronds fill an old vase and add a refined note to this impromptu woodland bistro.

THERE IS A GROWING MOVEMENT of like-minded camping aficionados who take to the road with their revitalized vintage campers that are fairly bursting with charm and newfound comfort. They are a group united by the idea that adding a dash of glamour to a camping trip is not just a romantic notion. Repurposed vintage lawn chairs, strings of twinkling lights, and mended colorful quilts — pulled from the recesses of their owners' linen cupboards — are packed up inside and then brought out to beautify the campsites upon arrival. Perfunctory canvas screen tents are passed over in favor of netting canopies strung from tree boughs, under which to sip cocktails or iced tea while enjoying nature with their fellow "glampers." We took the pesky task of mosquito control up a notch by repurposing a lacy vintage bedspread into an elegant bug screen by layering the material through an embroidery hoop and suspending it from a tree branch using lengths of simple twine.

READING NOOK
If the idea of camping—no matter how refined—doesn't appeal to you, then recreate this charming reading spot in your garden. Children, especially, will love the idea of creating a cozy nook like this where they can enjoy a book, daydream, watch butterflies, or giggle over shared secrets with a friend while enclosed in the lacy tent.

SUPPLIED BY NATURE

1. Add wild raspberries to any beverage for a hint of sweetness. **2.** Bring along a handmade journal to record memories and press fresh-picked leaves inside. **3.** Collect vegetation from nearby woods for art projects at home. **4.** A tiny wicker flask boasts a grassy bouquet.

FAIRY TALES
An ornamental birdhouse masquerades as a whimsical fairy cottage embellished with twigs, moss, and leaves plucked from the forest floor. Bring one along from your garden to entertain little campers

SUMMER KITCHEN

A side table (OPPOSITE)—cobbled together using scrap wood, sturdy twigs, and branches—is the perfect example of how salvaged pieces can be made from the humblest of materials. Use as an additional prep space when cooking up a traditional, hearty camper's breakfast of bacon, eggs, and muffins.

THIS PAGE: Create a casual outdoor camp kitchen for open-air cooking: **1.** A curved branch offers the perfect spot to hold a pretty apron. Recycled S-hooks from your garage can be used to hang enamel cooking pots and cooking implements. **2.** Another branch is put to use to hang a floral tote. **3.** Torn strips of fabric are repurposed as chair- back slipcovers. Simply wrap twine or jute around the fabric to secure.

BRIGHT IDEA
Campsite or garden lighting need not be boring. Re-use a discarded lampshade by fitting it with a stick-on battery-operated light. Attach the light to the top of the shade's frame and use twine to hang it from a tree.

Create this easy but elegant outdoor light fixture to boost the glow coming from the campfire—and help you see when marshmallow supplies are running low.

CAMP CHIC

Create your own flowering botanical pillow with a small fabric remnant, some acrylic craft paints, and a small selection of art brushes.

WHAT YOU'LL NEED:

- ○ 18 x 18-inch piece of fabric
- ○ Pink, white, and gold acrylic paint
- ○ ¾-inch oval glaze mop brush
- ○ Water
- ○ Iron
- ○ Scissors
- ○ 17 x 17-inch feather pillow form
- ○ Needle and thread

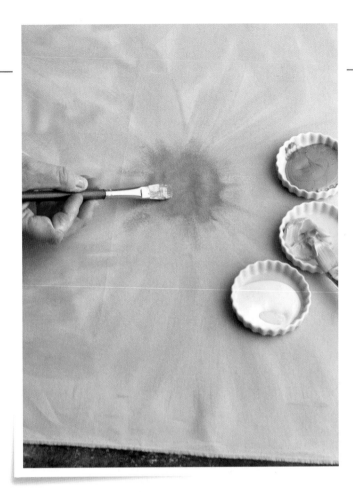

STEP ONE Using scissors, cut a piece of pink fabric to measure 18 x 18 inches. Iron the fabric flat. Place the fabric on a clean flat work surface.

STEP TWO To make the flowers, paint irregular flower centers on the right side of each fabric piece using gold paint. Let dry thoroughly (approx. 20 minutes). Once dry, apply petal-like strokes around the flower center to mimic a daisy. Let dry thoroughly.

STEP THREE Over the top of the daisy petal outlines, paint light strokes of white paint in smaller daisy petal shapes. Blend pink and white paints together with a small amount of water to give the white paint overlay a translucent effect. Let dry over night to let all paint layers cure fully.

STEP FOUR Stitch the two 18 x 18-inch painted fabric pieces inside out, leaving a 10-inch opening on one side to insert a feather pillow form. Turn the stitched pillow case right side out and insert the pillow form. Close the pillow opening using a basting stitch seam.

step-by-step
turn the tables

A $40 flea-market find ($30 after some friendly negotiation) becomes a living room asset thanks to an elegant paint finish. Here's how to do it yourself. Sorry, bargaining tips not included.

WHAT YOU'LL NEED:

- ○ Old table
- ○ Molding
- ○ Sandpaper
- ○ Tack cloth
- ○ Primer
- ○ Paint
- ○ Wood glue
- ○ Small clamps
- ○ Electrical tape

"This table was missing a leaf. At first, I thought I'd remove the other leaf to make a console, but decided it could sometimes be used as a cozy eating spot."
— Matthew

STEP ONE Before you buy a piece of furniture at a flea market or estate sale, give it a thorough exam. With a table, you want to look for sturdy legs, a flat top, and tight joints—meaning the table doesn't wobble. It's one thing to find a bargain that needs a bit of love, it's another to take on a huge project. This table fell into the former category. Strong and stable, the table just needed a new finish and something to address its missing extension leaf.

STEP TWO Measure the side of the table to determine what sizes of molding you will need to cover the raw edge of the table top, as well as the holes in the apron where the leaf use to be attached. Take these measurements to the home center, and find pieces of molding that will fit the table. For a small fee, the home center will cut the molding to length using your measurements.

STEP THREE The wide piece of molding fits the apron piece of the old table and covers the holes. "Since this would become the front of the table once I placed it against a wall," Matthew says, "I wanted something with decorative presence. The rope twist edge on this piece of molding ties in nicely with the fluted carvings in the table legs."

STEP FOUR To fill in the convex lip of the table top, which was left behind after the interlocking leaf was lost, choose a slender piece of molding with a rounded profile.

TIP: When redoing old furniture, primer is your best friend. It will seal old paint finishes, cover up blemishes and stains, and provide a smooth base for the paint to adhere to.

STEP FIVE After lightly sanding the molding to knock off any splinters, run a tack cloth over it to remove any dust. Then coat the molding with primer. "I like to use Bulls Eye 1-2-3® by Zinsser," Matthew says. "It's a water-base primer, so it's easy to clean up. And it seems to go over just about any finish." Later, you can use the same primer on the table.

STEP SIX It may take multiple coats of primer and paint to cover the old finish of a piece of secondhand furniture. In the case of this table, two coats of primer sealed up the original stain so it wouldn't bleed through the topcoat. Then, apply the paint of your choosing. "I picked a shade of gray called 'Adobe' by Pratt & Lambert," Matthew says.

STEP SEVEN Paint the molding pieces to match the table.

STEP EIGHT With a light hand, apply wood glue to the back of the piece of molding. Too much glue will spill out and make a mess. Wipe up any excess glue before it dries.

STEP NINE For the lightweight piece of trim molding, all that's needed to hold it in place is a piece of tape. Matthew used electrical tape, which won't mar the paint finish, but you can also use blue painter's tape. Leave the tape in place until the glue dries, which is anywhere from 2 to 24 hours, depending on the humidity in the air. "Just to be safe, I left it in place overnight," Matthew says.

STEP TEN Using the same light hand and a back-and-forth motion, apply wood glue to the back of the large piece of molding.

STEP ELEVEN Use clamps to hold the heavier piece of molding in place until the glue dries.

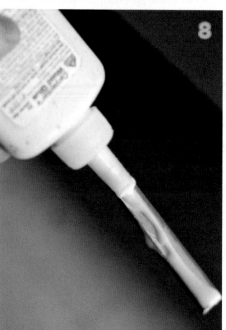

STEP TWELVE With the leaf folded down, the table is a wall-hugging console table that attractively displays collectibles. With the leaf extended, the table becomes a casual eating spot perfect for a tight space, such as a small kitchen or living room. Set it and enjoy!

SECOND TIME AROUND

With a soft spot for items from the past and a talent for repurposing almost everything, antiques dealer Donna Welch opens her home to share her heartfelt and inventive approach to decorating with vintage finds.

ABOVE AND BEYOND
A mix of old clocks (OPPOSITE) and clock faces makes a graphic and functional collection. In Donna's simple dining room (THIS PAGE), an array of country-style finds tethered to a tobacco drying rack creates interest overhead

KNOWN FOR HER FONDNESS for old-fashioned country ingenuity, antiques shop owner Donna Welch highlights rural wares in her Goffstown, New Hampshire, businesses as well as in her 18th-century farmhouse home. Her love of old painted wood and rustic farm implements—and her uncanny ability to meld several of these elements together to create a new and useful item—is the hallmark of her deeply personal style. Her home, which is just steps from her stylish and bustling shop, is filled with her favorite finds—all cleverly cobbled together in ways that are both interesting and unique. "I find second, third, and fourth uses for everything I collect," Donna says. "These items are well-made and have stood the test of time." Visitors to her shop, From Out of the Woods, know they will encounter items that will help them establish or embellish vintage-inspired décor. At the same time, they gather Donna's ideas for ways to use the antiques. "If you are going to live with something that is centuries old, it must inspire you with its design, while at the same time earning its keep," Donna says. Collectibles that Donna sees as infused with purpose are called out in a special section of her shop, INFUSION NH.

Donna's home is also her experimental laboratory. Many of the items that end up for sale in her shop begin as implements in her home. She especially likes to layer and stack pieces in multiple sizes, colors, and shapes, building artful sculptures that pay homage to the craftsmanship and uniqueness of the old wares. "When you recycle a mix of antiques into a decorative display, it means that no one else will have exactly what you have created yourself," she says.

PUTTING IT ALL TOGETHER

A mix of storage boxes and kneelers from the turn of the century create a colorful montage atop the living room mantle (ABOVE, RIGHT). A downstairs bathroom (OPPOSITE) is a feast of reuse ideas: A panel door is decorative focal point and a spot to hang a mirror. The rung of a chair becomes a towel holder, and a vintage basket is a place for light laundry. The vanity is made of an old wooden commode retrofitted with modern plumbing. Donna used an early peg board as a backsplash and a place to show off quirky finds.

ODE TO ORGANIZATION

Mini chests of drawers are as useful today as they were in the past as ways to organize hardware, spices, and apothecary needs. Massed together on one wall they are visual reminders of the the rural wisdom of "a place for everything and everything in its place."

PRETTY AND PRACTICAL

Vintage items get new appreciation in Donna's house. **1.** Vintage table legs are sophisticated candle holders on a table made from a grind stone. **2.** When unhooked from the rack above the dining table where it displays messages, a cast-iron fire place griddle can perform as a cutting and serving board. **3.** A vintage porch column becomes a coat hanger with the addition of old metal school hooks. **4.** Boxes corral and store tablets, remotes, and other electronics in the living room.

ART AND UTILITY

"Nothing is free from re-interpertation," Donna says. **1.** A tractor wheel mounted on the wall is eye-catching art. **2.** She uses a vintage Norton hens-and-chicks planter to hold kitchen implements. **3.** Donna envisioned turning a vintage wooden boat into a seating piece, and her husband Tom made it happen. The edge of the hull becomes a console table. **4.** French linen panels cover the cushions.

When you open your eyes,
heart, and mind, everything
has multiple ways to rock this
world as something else.
— Donna Welch

SEE SAW

An industrial table-saw base topped with a piece of butcher block is an extra work surface in Donna's kitchen. Currently, it displays an old drawer she turned into a caddy by adding thick rope handles. More rope wrapped around pickle jars and a bottle turn them into textural sculpture.

IN THE DETAILS

In Donna's house, as in her store, every item has new purpose and appeal.
1. A glass jar topped with a car battery case cover becomes a handy kitchen string holder. **2.** A rustic pogo stick horse head is instant sculpture. **3.** Years ago, someone repaired this strainer with wire, and the result is a charming conversation piece. **4.** Mounted to the wall, a painted wood trough becomes a shelf for early decorative crockery. **5.** Donna tucks flowers into a vase and nestles them in an old leather fire bucket. **6.** Pounded-flat utensils decorate the edge of a hand-loomed linen table runner. **7.** Old doll furniture hangs from a rustic peg rack in the bathroom. **8.** Wire garden fencing and a pie-tin cover turn a pickle jar into a unique storage canister.

NEW WAYS WITH OLD WARES

Donna creates inventive home accessories out of vintage objects and found items. Here's how to recreate some of her favorites for your home. You can also find similar items at her store: From Out of the Woods/Infusion NH in Goffstown, New Hampshire (601/624-8668).

WHAT YOU'LL NEED:

- Chair rung
- Door knob
- Tin pie plate
- Egg basket
- Broken compass parts
- Rope, various thicknesses
- Glue gun

- Heavy-weight paper
- Empty jars without lids
- Scraps of cloth
- Tins
- Wooden disks
- Wire

1

2

STEP ONE Drill holes in both ends of the chair rung—a narrow hole in one end and a wide one in the other. Place the rung in the middle of the pie plate with the narrow hole against the pie plate, and drill a flat-head screw through the plate into the hole. Place a door knob into the wide hole.

STEP TWO Tie a square knot at the base of the basket to start. Weave in and out of the wire supports. Tie off with another square knot. If desired, weave thinner rope in a braid or macramé pattern to cover the handle.

STEP THREE Wrap thick rope around the base of the compass, using hot glue to secure the coils, and knot the ends. Cut a circle of heavy-weight paper or cardboard the same diameter as the coil, and glue it to the underside. Insert a tea light.

STEP FOUR Use your imagination to meld items, including tins and wood disks, to fashion lids for leftover jars. Poke holes in the tins using an awl, and insert loops of wire. Or coil a tight roll out of fabric scraps and hot-glue ends to secure.

ALL DYED UP

Personalize vintage fabrics, textiles, and clothing with your own unique palette. Follow the steps of these easy dyeing techniques and choose your favorite hues.

BEFORE & AFTER

An assortment of vintage table linens and a plain new towel show off fresh looks in delicious new colors (THIS PAGE). Visit a fabric or crafts store—or shop similar sites online—to find fiber-reactive dyes. DharmaTrading.com is one such web site, and it offers a rainbow of colors (OPPOSITE).

COLOR PLAY

Mouthwatering shades (THIS PAGE). Tinted yarn, twine, and string (OPPOSITE, LEFT). Plain fabrics awaiting makeovers (OPPOSITE, RIGHT).

IF YOU'RE A STICKLER FOR EXACTNESS AND PRECISION, textile and fiber dyeing isn't for you. It's a fluid and organic process that often yields results different from what you expected. Which is exactly why Matthew loves it: "There are no guarantees to the final shade created," he says. "I like the serendipitous nature of it and enjoy the surprise at the end." The final hue, no matter how unpredictable, is beautiful, soft, and earthy—and unlike anything you can find in a store. Taking a plain white piece of cotton or linen, and dipping it in the bowl full of color transforms it into something unique and personal. You can control how vivid the hue is by how long you let the fabric swirl around in the liquid. You can play with different shades—even create something truly new—by how many dyes you expose the fabric to. Shop secondhand stores for clothing, scarves, or shoes. Grab a pile of linens from a table at a flea market. Unspool a skein of yarn or seam binding. And enjoy the process.

TEXTILE TIPS

Test a swatch of your fiber or textile first to make sure it will accept dye. It won't if it has:

- 50 percent or more polyester content
- Bleach damage
- A label that says "Dry Clean Only"
- Water-repellent finish

DYE TRICKS

Pre-wash your fabric for best results. Read the directions that come with the dye kits. A typical recipe includes:

- Powdered dye
- Soda ash
- Non-Iodized Salt
- Water

CRAFTED BY HAND

There's tremendous satisfaction in taking a plain, colorless piece of fabric and transforming it. **1.** To make this checkerboard, start with a 16x16-inch square of linen or cotton. Dye it a dark shade of your choosing. Then, use a square sponge to stamp on fabric paint in a light shade. For the checkers, use leftover fabric to cover buttons. **2.** Dye vintage or new linen napkins, then embellish a corner with a fabric-covered button in a different shade. **3.** After dyeing towels, wash them as normal, and use fabric softener to renew their fluffiness.

OPPOSITE: A new lilac shade sets off the embroidery of this tea towel. Feature the design by draping it over a desk, vanity, or shelf edge.

OUR PALETTE

We used the following fiber-reactive dyes from DharmaTrading.com to create the projects on these pages:

• PR15	• PR49
• PR16	• PR61
• PR17	• PR86
• PR38A	• PR112

Spring is the perfect season to dye fabrics: Take galvanized metal buckets of dye outdoors, and use a clothes rack or line to dry the items.

MIXOLOGY

This array of linen pieces shows the variations you can achieve with textile dye. Add more dye to the mix or let the fabric soak longer for darker colors. Or, dip the fabric into one hue and then into another to get a blend of shades.

INSPIRATION POINTS

Try one of these ideas: **1.** Finger-weave dyed twine into long friendship bracelets to drape around bottles. **2.** Color cocktail napkins to match your décor. **3.** Dress up any meal with linen placemats in vivid hues. **4.** Sew bits of a dyed thrift-store shirt into glasses cases.

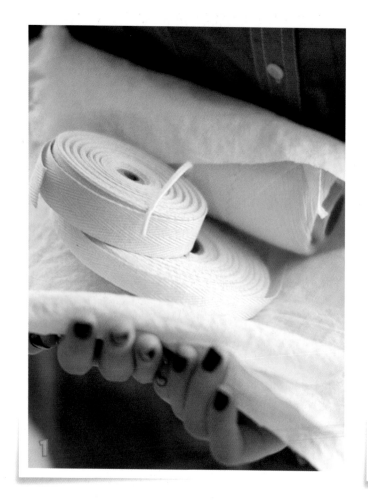

BASIC DYEING STEPS

This is a good introduction to textile dyeing. As you get more advanced, you can move onto trickier fibers, such as wool, silk, and even suede.

WHAT YOU'LL NEED:

- Prewashed all-cotton or all-linen fabrics
- Powdered Dye
- Hot water (Several tablespoons plus 1 gallon)
- Small glass dish
- Large glass or metal bowl or bucket
- Non-iodized salt, such as kosher salt or water-softener salt
- Soda ash (1 ounce is needed per gallon)
- Latex or rubber gloves (optional but recommended)

STEP ONE To get even absorption of dye and no streaks or spots, it's necessary to pre-wash your fabric to remove any soil or grease. Do not add fabric softener to the wash. Dry the fabric. If you machine-dry it, do not use dryer sheets.

STEP TWO In the small glass dish, make a slurry by mixing your fabric dye and several tablespoons of hot water. Follow the manufacturer's directions for the recommended amount of dye for 1 gallon of water. Stir the slurry into a gallon of water in the large bowl or bucket. Add the required amount of non-iodized salt into the dye bath and stir to dissolve completely.

STEP THREE Add the fabric. Stir gently and frequently for at least 20 minutes, or until you achieve the color intensity you want. Leave it in for less time to get a lighter shade, for more time to get a deeper shade. To set the color, add a fixative, such as soda ash. In the small glass dish, make a slurry of water and soda ash, which you can buy at fabric and crafts stores. Slowly add it to the dye bath, being careful not to dump it on the fabric itself. Let the fabric soak for another 20 to 30 minutes, stirring occasionally.

STEP FOUR As long as the fibers are all natural and unvarnished, you can dye nearly any textile, from ribbons to seam binding, string to swim towels, shirts to canvas shoes.

STEP FIVE Rinse the fabric in cold water until the fabric is the desired shade.

STEP SIX Wring out the fabric to remove as much excess water as possible. If the fabric is too saturated and allowed to drip dry, water rivulets will create drip lines in the finish.

STEP SEVEN Let the fabric dry on a clothes rack or line. After this, wash it separately from other loads the first two times.

TIP: Start with really hot tap water. If you don't get the intense colors you are looking for, or if your textile is thick and dense, create the dye bath in a stockpot on the stove. Keep the dye bath hot over low flame while you work.

STRAWBERRY MINI-TARTS

YOU WILL NEED:

- ❍ 1-2 pints fresh strawberries
- ❍ Strawberry sauce (SEE BELOW)

FOR THE TART SHELLS:

- ❍ 1 cup flour
- ❍ ½ teaspoon salt
- ❍ ⅓ cup plus 1 Tablespoon shortening
- ❍ 2 to 3 Tablespoons cold water

Preheat oven to 400° F

1. In a medium bowl, combine flour and salt. Cut in shortening with a fork or pastry blender until the mixture resembles coarse crumbs. Sprinkle in water until dough forms and is easy to ball and remove from the bowl.

2. On a lightly floured surface, roll the dough until it is ¼-inch thick. Using a biscuit cutter, drinking glass, or circle cookie cutter, cut 12 circles. Place them in mini-tart pan.

3. Bake for 10 to 12 minutes or until golden. Let cool.

4. Fill tart shells with fresh strawberries and drizzle with strawberry sauce.

STRAWBERRY SAUCE

YOU WILL NEED:

- ❍ 1 pint fresh strawberries, hulled
- ❍ ¼ cup granulated sugar, or more to taste
- ❍ 4 Tablespoons water, divided
- ❍ ½ teaspoon balsamic vinegar
- ❍ 1 teaspoon cornstarch

1. Combine strawberries, sugar, 2 tablespoons of water, and balsamic vinegar in a saucepan and bring to simmer over medium heat.

2. Reduce heat to medium-low, cover, and simmer for 15 minutes.

3. Whisk together 2 tablespoons water and the cornstarch in a small bowl.

4. Whisk cornstarch mixture into strawberry mixture. Cook, stirring constantly, until mixture thickens, 1 to 2 minutes. Remove from heat.

5. Let mixture cool, then transfer to a blender and purée until smooth.

CHERRY SHORTCAKE

YOU WILL NEED:

- ❍ 6 cups Bing cherries, pitted and halved
- ❍ 6 Tablespoons plus ¼ cup granulated sugar
- ❍ Zest of 2 lemons
- ❍ 2 cups all-purpose flour
- ❍ 2 teaspoons cream of tartar
- ❍ 1 teaspoon baking soda
- ❍ 1 teaspoon ground cinnamon
- ❍ 1 teaspoon ground cardamom
- ❍ ½ teaspoon salt
- ❍ ½ cup butter, cut into cubes and frozen
- ❍ 1 egg, beaten
- ❍ ½ cup cold half-and-half, or more as needed
- ❍ 1 egg white (optional)
- ❍ 1 teaspoon granulated sugar, or to taste
- ❍ 1 cup whipped cream
- ❍ 2 Tablespoons poppy seeds

Preheat oven to 425° F

1. Line a baking sheet with parchment paper.

2. Combine cherries, 6 tablespoons sugar, and lemon zest in a bowl. Set aside and allow cherries to rest for 2 to 3 hours.

3. Mix flour, ¼ cup sugar, cream of tartar, baking soda, cinnamon, cardamom, and salt in a large bowl. Cut in butter with a fork or pastry blender until the mixture resembles coarse crumbs.

4. Whisk egg and half-and-half in a small bowl; stir into the flour mixture with a fork until dough is moistened with large clumps. (Add a teaspoon more half-and-half to the bowl if dough won't come together.)

5. Roll tennis-ball-size scoops of dough and place on prepared baking sheet. Press each ball down lightly to form ½-inch-thick discs. Brush dough with egg white and sprinkle with 1 teaspoon sugar.

6. Bake until golden brown, 12 to 14 minutes. Cool in the pan for 10 minutes before removing to cool completely on a wire rack.

7. Slice each cake in half horizontally. Layer cherries and whipped cream between cake halves. Top with another dollop of whipped cream and a sprinkle of poppy seeds, and garnish with a whole cherry if desired.

RECIPES

STRAWBERRY BREAD

YOU WILL NEED:

- 2 cups of strawberries, hulled and sliced
- 1 cup granulated sugar, divided
- 1 ½ cups all-purpose flour
- 1 teaspoon baking powder
- ½ teaspoon baking soda
- ½ teaspoon cinnamon
- ¼ teaspoon salt
- 2 large eggs
- ¼ cup melted margarine, melted and cooled
- ¼ cup applesauce

Preheat oven to 350° F.

1. Grease and flour a 9 x 5 x 3-inch loaf pan.

2. Place the strawberries in a bowl and sprinkle with ½ cup of the sugar.

3. In a large bowl, blend together the remaining sugar, the flour, baking powder, baking soda, salt, and cinnamon.

4. In a medium bowl, beat the eggs until foamy. Then beat in the margarine and the applesauce. Stir in the strawberries. Combine the two mixtures, blending until the dry ingredients are moistened.

5. Scrape the batter into the prepared pan and bake for 45 to 55 minutes, or until a cake tester inserted into the center comes out clean and the top is golden. Remove from the oven and cool the pan on a wire rack for 5-10 minutes before removing the loaf from the pan.

6. If desired, serve with spread of cream cheese and strawberry sauce (see recipe on previous page).

BLUEBERRY BARS

YOU WILL NEED:

- 3½ cups all-purpose flour
- 6 Tablespoons granulated sugar
- 1 cup butter, cut into cubes

FOR THE BLUEBERRY TOPPING:

- 6 cups fresh blueberries
- ¾ cup brown sugar
- ½ cup all-purpose flour
- ½ cup cold, unsalted butter cut into cubes
- 2 teaspoons cinnamon
- 4 Tablespoons tangerine juice or the juice of a fresh orange.

Preheat oven 350° F

1. Line a 12 x 17-inch rimmed baking sheet pan with parchment paper. Set aside.

2. In a large bowl, stir together flour and sugar. Cut in 1 cup butter with a fork or pastry blender until the mixture resembles coarse crumbs. Using your hands, form a ball of dough and knead until smooth.

3. Press the dough evenly into the pan using your fingers.

4. In a medium bowl, mix blueberries, brown sugar, ½ cup flour, ½ cup butter, and cinnamon. Toss well, and then add tangerine juice. Stir gently to mix.

5. Spread the berries mixture over the dough.

6. Bake for 30-35 minutes, or until some of the berries have burst and made a sauce. Cool for one hour.

7. Cut into squares and serve with ice cream or whipped cream.

FREE-CYCLE

Found sea urchin shells make excellent candleholders. Wash and rinse them, then insert tall thin tapers for your next special celebration.